AF223344

EINZELSCHRIFTEN

Wolf Hoffmann
Turnaround Equity – Erfolgsfaktoren im Transaktionsprozess
bei Turnaround-Investitionen in Deutschland
Lohmar – Köln 2011 ◆ 256 S. ◆ € 57,- (D) ◆ ISBN 978-3-8441-0017-4

Christoph Zulehner
**Strategisches Führen in Gesundheits- und Pflegeunter-
nehmen** – Handbuch für die Praxis
Lohmar – Köln 2011 ◆ 272 S. ◆ € 35,- (D) ◆ ISBN 978-3-8441-0018-1

Mirko Mertenskötter
**Qualität, Vertrauen und Akzeptanz im Kontext der Internen
Revision**
Lohmar – Köln 2011 ◆ 368 S. ◆ € 64,- (D) ◆ ISBN 978-3-8441-0019-8

Jan Breitweg
Planung, Finanzierung und Management von Kunstfonds –
Eine empirische Analyse
Lohmar – Köln 2011 ◆ 252 S. ◆ € 57,- (D) ◆ ISBN 978-3-8441-0027-3

Patrick Kraus
**Die Auswirkung von Corporate Governance und Nachhaltig-
keit auf den Unternehmenserfolg** – Eine Betrachtung im Kontext der wertorientierten Unternehmensführung
Lohmar – Köln 2011 ◆ 176 S. ◆ € 48,- (D) ◆ ISBN 978-3-8441-0028-0

Dennis Schlegel
**Subsidiary Controlling with Strategically Aligned
Performance Measurement Systems**
Lohmar – Köln 2011 ◆ 140 S. ◆ € 43,- (D) ◆ ISBN 978-3-8441-0030-3

Stefan Karenfort
Synergy in Mergers & Acquisitions – The Role of Business
Relatedness
Lohmar – Köln 2011 ◆ 148 S. ◆ € 43,- (D) ◆ ISBN 978-3-8441-0035-8

JOSEF EUL VERLAG

Dr. Stefan Karenfort

Synergy in Mergers & Acquisitions

The Role of Business Relatedness

Bibliografische Information der Deutschen Nationalbibliothek

Die Deutsche Nationalbibliothek verzeichnet diese Publikation
in der Deutschen Nationalbibliografie; detaillierte bibliografische
Daten sind im Internet über <http://dnb.d-nb.de> abrufbar.

ISBN 978-3-8441-0035-8
1. Auflage Mai 2011

© JOSEF EUL VERLAG GmbH, Lohmar – Köln, 2011
Alle Rechte vorbehalten

JOSEF EUL VERLAG GmbH
Brandsberg 6
53797 Lohmar
Tel.: 0 22 05 / 90 10 6-6
Fax: 0 22 05 / 90 10 6-88
E-Mail: info@eul-verlag.de
http://www.eul-verlag.de

**Bei der Herstellung unserer Bücher möchten wir die Umwelt schonen. Dieses
Buch ist daher auf säurefreiem, 100% chlorfrei gebleichtem, alterungsbestän-
digem Papier nach DIN 6738 gedruckt.**

Acknowledgements

I would like to extend my sincere gratitude to my supervisor Dr. Lim Cheng Hwa for his guidance and encouragement throughout all stages of the research project. I am also thankful to Mr. Weidner who made it possible to conduct the survey within the IMAP organization. In addition, I would like to acknowledge Ms. Hiltrud Niggemann who has provided support with the statistical analysis. The final draft of this thesis has been edited by Dr. Guenter Plum.

Acknowledgements

Table of Contents

List of Figures

List of Tables

Abbreviations

FTC	Federal Trade Commission
IMAP	International Mergers & Acquisition Partners
M&A	Mergers and Acquisitions
R&D	Research and Development
ROI	Return on Investment
S.D.	Standard Deviation
SEC	Securities and Exchange Commission
SIC	Standard Industrial Classification
USD	United States Dollar
VIF	Variance Inflation Factors

1 Introduction

The subject research project resides in the field of mergers & acquisitions (M&A). In the past decades, M&A have been well established as an important strategic tool for firms worldwide (Rappaport 1986, p. 198). During the period 1995-2008, the global M&A transaction volume has increased at an average annual growth rate of 9.2% from 807 bn USD in 1995 to 2,530 bn USD in 2008 which underpins the increasing importance of M&A worldwide (Tschöke and Klemen 2010) (see figure 1-1).

Figure 1-1: Global M&A transaction volume 1995-2009

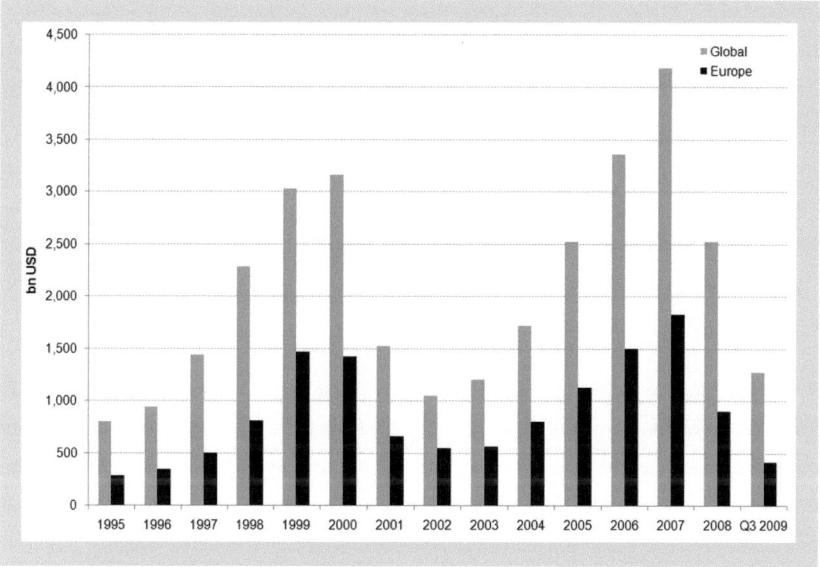

Source: Adapted from Tschöke and Klemen 2010, p. 83

Essentially, acquisitions resemble the purchase of a bundle of assets and technologies and therefore constitute a capital budgeting decision. Acquirers often pay a premium over the market value of these assets and technologies in pursuit of synergy (Sirower 1997, p. 4). The term synergy can be defined as the "increase in performance of the combined firm over what the two firms are already expected or required to accomplish as independent firms" (Sirower 1997, p. 20). The phenomenon of synergy is often illustrated as the "2+2=5-effect" (Ansoff 1965, p. 75). However, unlike major capital expenditures, M&A projects do not provide the option to conduct trial runs, as the entire purchase price including any acquisition premium is usually agreed and paid up front. Moreover, M&A are very difficult to reverse, particularly once the post-merger integration has commenced (Sirower 1997, p. 6). Therefore, M&A have major long-term implications for the fate of the acquiring and target firms.

As a result, considerable attention has been given by the academic community to studying the determining factors of M&A success (Lubatkin 1983; Shleifer and Vishny 1988; Chatterjee 1992; Datta, Pinches and Narayanan 1992; Sirower 1997; Bruner 2004). In management research, two major streams of inquiry have evolved. One stream investigates how far the *strategic fit* between the merging firms will impact future performance, whereby the term strategic fit depicts the degree of shared technologies between the merging firms. The other stream of research elicits the impact of *cultural fit* between the merging firms on the financial success of the combination (Chatterjee, Lubatkin, Schweiger and Weber 1992, p. 319).

1.1   Introduction to the research

The realization of synergy is a dominant objective of acquirers to pursue M&A (Mukherjee, Kiymaz and Baker 2004). At the same time, synergy is often critical for the overall success of M&A, in particular if the acquirer has paid a premium over the market value of the target firm (KPMG 2006, p. 2). Hence, this research project will focus on the critical factors which influence the creation of synergy in M&A.

In this context, researchers have extensively studied the impact of the strategic fit. The relevant literature has strongly relied on the basic intuition that strategic relatedness between the merging firms should facilitate synergy and thus increase post-merger performance (Sirower 1997, p. 90). As highlighted by Bruner (2004, p. 69), "executives intuitively understand that acquiring peer competitors offers opportunities for cost savings, asset reductions, and other efficiencies".

In the early stages, the strategic relatedness has been conceptualized as the presence of similarities concerning product-/market attributes between the previously
independent firms (Chatterjee 1986; Lubatkin 1987; Singh and Montgomery 1987).
In the more recent time, the focus of inquiry shifted from product-/market relatedness
to a *resource-based view* (Wernerfelt 1984) considering similarities and differences
of the resource configuration between the merging entities (Harrison, Hitt, Hoskisson
and Ireland 1991; Hitt, Harrison, Ireland and Best 1998). Furthermore, not only
similarities and differences between the merging firms, but also complementarities
were considered as determining factors for the realization of synergy and M&A success (Larsson and Finkelstein 1999). The findings from a large number of research
projects are however conflicting and do not provide a conclusive explanation as to
the effectiveness of strategic relatedness on synergy realization and M&A performance (Sirower 1997, p. 90; Bruner 2004, p. 69).

1.2   Justification and objective of the research

The incoherent evidence concerning the impact of strategic relatedness on M&A
performance is partly attributed to weaknesses in the measurement of the underlying
concept. Many research projects have measured relatedness as a dichotomous
variable and therefore did not consider the degree of relatedness (Sirower 1997, p.
90). Besides, it has been highlighted that most measurement approaches, such as
product-count measures or merger classifications, apply an external view to the firm.
Thus, strategic considerations which are essential for the decision-making of managers are neglected entirely (Pehrsson 2006b, p. 355).

Traditionally, studies in the field of M&A have relied on a narrow measurement of
relatedness based on a limited number of product/market or resource attributes.
More recent contributions advocate a multi-dimensional concept of relatedness
based on managerial perceptions (Stimpert and Duhaime 1997; Pehrsson 2006a;
Pehrsson 2006b). So far, this measurement approach has only been applied to study
the impact of relatedness on the performance of diversified firms and foreign subsidiaries (Pehrsson 2006a; Pehrsson 2009). The proposed study shall attempt to

enhance the understanding of the impact of relatedness on synergy realization by applying the measurement approach to the field of M&A. It is also planned to elicit the planning accuracy and effectiveness of negative synergy which appears to be neglected by many acquiring firms (Early 2004). Furthermore, there is empirical evidence that the impact of relatedness is influenced by the speed of the post-merger integration project which so far has received little attention (Homburg and Bucerius 2006).

The proposed research project, which is conducted as a quantitative survey with M&A consultants in 39 countries world-wide, shall therefore address this gap in research by investigating the impact of relatedness on M&A performance using a multi-dimensional measure based on managerial perceptions. In contrast to earlier studies, the performance effects of different attributes of relatedness are considered simultaneously from a perspective familiar with the internal decision-making processes of the firm. The research project will not only consider a single measure of M&A performance in line with most contributions in the field, but will focus on the important phenomenon of synergy realization, considering separately, the performance contributions derived from income and cost efficiencies.

The research questions which shall be addressed within the research project are as follows:

1. To what extent does business relatedness impact synergy in M&A?

2. To what extent does the speed of the post-merger integration project influence synergy realization?

3. What is the planning accuracy and effectiveness of dyssynergy?

4. What is the impact of diversification on M&A performance?

The objective of the research project is to provide a better understanding of the performance implications of M&A based on the relatedness between the acquiring and the target firm. In particular, the study shall enable corporate managers to make predictions about the synergistic potential which are often critical for the success of M&A. The performance impact of the speed of the post-merger integration phase is also investigated in conjunction with relatedness. As a result, the study will provide a valuable insight into the performance implications of the pace of the integration project for different configurations of relatedness. In addition to the benefits for corporate executives, the research project shall revisit and advance the academic discussion on relatedness and M&A performance by adopting a new measurement approach from diversification research to the field of M&A and synergy management.

1.3   Overview of the thesis

First, the study shall provide an overview on the relevant literature. At the outset, the prevailing theories will be introduced explaining the phenomenon of M&A, including the efficiency theory which posits that M&A are realized in pursuit of synergy (Trautwein 1990). The basic principles of M&A valuation will be considered including the relationship between the acquisition premium and the synergistic potential. The concept of synergy as well as different synergy types and their effectiveness will be discussed. Finally, there will be a focus on the relationship between business relatedness and M&A performance. Different approaches to measuring the degree of relatedness will be introduced and their strengths and weakness are discussed. Findings of past research projects studying the impact of business relatedness on M&A performance will be reviewed and the key findings summarized and discussed. The gap in contemporary research will be highlighted.

Second, will be a discussion of the research methodology applied in the study. Given that the research project is based on a quantitative hypothesis-testing research design, the conceptual model and the individual variables will be introduced. Thereafter, the research questions and hypotheses will be formulated based on the extant literature. The sampling approach and the online questionnaire survey, which is the research instrument used in the research project, shall be discussed. The data analysis approach will be elaborated, based on various bivariate and multivariate statistical tests, such as analysis of variance and multiple-regression analysis. The methodology chapter will be concluded with a discussion on reliability and validity concerns, as well as ethical considerations.

Third, the results of the research project will be presented. A profile of the respondents will be provided using univariate statistics, such as frequency distributions. A correlation matrix will illustrate the relationship between the individual variables. Thereafter, the hypotheses will be tested using different multivariate statistics. Last, the study will conclude with a summary of key findings and a discussion of the implications for theory and practice. Suggestions for future research will be proposed.

2   Literature review

This chapter provides an overview on the extant literature pertaining to the study. First, relevant theories to explain the phenomenon of M&A will be reviewed. Second, the concept and effectiveness of synergy in M&A will be introduced. Third, the concept of relatedness and its relevance for synergy and post-merger performance will be discussed.

2.1   Motives for Mergers & Acquisitions

A significant amount of research has been conducted on the motives of M&A. Based on the extant literature, it appears appropriate to distinguish between three broad categories of theories to explain the phenomenon of M&A, namely i) economic motives, ii) managerial motives and iii) financial motives (Hofmann 2004, pp. 167-185).

2.1.1   Economic Motives

The relevant economic theories, namely those of efficiency and monopoly, have in common that M&A result in an incremental value for the merging parties, i.e. the beneficiaries of M&A are both the shareholders of the acquiring and the target company (Rodermann 1999, p. 54; Hofmann 2004, p. 168).

2.1.1.1   Efficiency Theory

The efficiency theory posits that M&A are executed to achieve "net gains from synergies" (Trautwein 1990, p. 284). More specifically, the efficiency gains accrue from operating synergies which are achieved through the transfer of knowledge as well as from economies of scale and economies of scope (Rodermann 1999, p. 55). According to the synergy hypothesis, efficiency gains are not generic in nature but rather peculiar to two specific firms coming together (Mueller and Sirower 2003, p. 375). Various empirical studies confirm that synergy is a dominant motive for practitioners to engage in M&A (Berkovitch and Narayanan 1993; Mukherjee et al. 2004). The concept of synergy will be discussed in more detail later in this thesis.

2.1.1.2   Monopoly Theory

According to the monopoly theory, M&A are realized in order to achieve a monopoly rent through increased market power. The monopoly theory is an explanation for horizontal and conglomerate M&A. Market power can be accomplished through the deliberate reduction of supply, cross-subsidizing products and deterring potential market entrants (Trautwein 1990, p. 286; Rodermann 1999, p. 137). These benefits are also referred to as collusive synergy (Chatterjee 1986, p. 121) and competitor interrelationships (Porter 1985, p. 353).

2.1.2 Managerial Motives

There are three theories which can be grouped under managerial motives for M&A, namely i) the inefficient management theory, ii) the managerial discretion theory and iii) the hubris theory. All theories take it as given that the purpose of engaging in M&A is related to managerial qualifications and objectives.

2.1.2.1   Inefficient Management Theory

The inefficient management theory, which is also referred to as the market for corporate control theory (Manne 1965), is based on the notion that the incumbent management of a specific firm is not capable of capturing the full value potential due to lack of knowledge or qualification (Hofmann 2004, p. 174). The inefficient management can be replaced by a more competent management through M&A leading to an increment in shareholder value. As compared to the synergy theory, which requires two specific firms with a certain fit to be joined, basically any firm can capture the potential value gains according to the market for corporate control theory, by replacing the inefficient management with one of average competence (Mueller and Sirower 2003, p. 375).

2.1.2.2   Managerial Discretion Theory

A central justification of managerial motives is the principal-agent theory (Eisenhardt 1989) which explains that a firm's management (agent) may pursue personal objectives which are different to those of the shareholder (principal). Personal objectives may be the desire to enhance personal reputation, to increase financial compensation, as well as to accomplish a lasting legacy which is also referred to as empire building (Trautwein 1990, p. 287). Since these goals are often linked with the size of the firm, managers may resort to M&A to grow the company as a means to realizing their personal objectives (Rodermann 1999, p. 59).

2.1.2.3   Hubris Theory

The hubris theory constitutes a psychological-based approach to explain M&A. The theory posits that the management of the acquiring firm overrates their ability to evaluate potential acquisition targets. This managerial over-optimism typically results in erroneous decisions and M&A which are overpriced (Trautwein 1990, p. 289). "Potential bids are abandoned whenever the acquiring firm's valuation of the target turns up with a figure below the current market price. Bids are rendered when the valuation exceeds the price" (Roll 1986, p.212). Managerial hubris is likely to surface in a competitive auction in which the firm with the highest bid will close the deal. The risk of a potential failure, due to an overrated acquisition price which significantly exceeds the fair value of the target company, increases in an auction. This phenomenon is the basis of the winner's curse hypothesis which argues that the value of a target traded in an auction is usually lower than the acquisition price (Hofmann 2004, p. 178).

2.1.3 Financial Motives

Financial approaches to explain the phenomenon of M&A are based on the principal agent theory and the portfolio theory (Markowitz 1952). They share the premise that M&A are realized based on financial goals and not due to personal and performance objectives (Hofmann 2004, p. 179).

2.1.3.1   Valuation Theory

The valuation theory is based on the assumption of inefficient capital markets and asymmetric information. The goal of M&A is to achieve arbitrary value gains between the market value and the valuation of the acquiring firm as a result of unique information about the target company which is only available to the bidder's management (Rodermann 1999, p. 58).

2.1.3.2   Risk Diversification Theory

The risk diversification theory is based on the portfolio theory which assumes that an investor can reduce portfolio risk by holding a diversified portfolio of assets which are not perfectly correlated. Correspondingly, M&A enables the acquiring firm to diversify its activities and reduce the volatility of cash flows at a group level while maintaining the same level of returns (Hofmann 2004, p. 180).

Figure 2-1: M&A motives and relevant theories

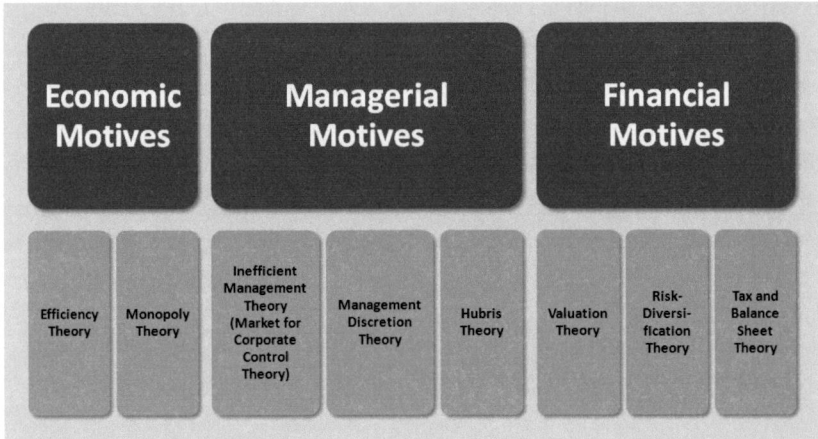

Source: Adapted from Hofmann 2004, p. 167

2.1.3.3   Tax and Balance Sheet Theory

The tax and balance sheet theory argues that M&A are realized in order to capture benefits from a restructuring of the financing and balance sheet of the combined entity. Furthermore, M&A can be motivated by benefits arising from offsetting tax profits and losses of the previously independent firms and which may also comprise the tax deductibility of the financing cost for the purchase price (Hofmann 2004, p.

183). The different motives and underlying theories regarding M&A are summarized in figure 2-1.

2.2 Synergy in Mergers & Acquisitions

Amongst practitioners, the phenomenon of synergy is often associated with M&A. A survey conducted with 636 American CFOs (final sample 75; response ratio 11.8%) shows that the realization of synergy is a dominant motive to engage in M&A, which underscores the relevance of the efficiency theory (Mukherjee et al. 2004).

In fact, the success of M&A is significantly dependent on the synergies realized, as is apparent from a study by KPMG (2006) with 101 corporate executives.

> *Nearly two thirds of companies whose deal enhanced value met or exceeded their internal synergy and performance improvement targets. Conversely, 73 percent of companies whose deal reduced value, failed to meet their synergy and performance improvement targets (KPMG 2006, p. 2).*

Many acquirers fail to meet the planned synergy targets set during the pre-merger evaluation as also shown by the results of a customer survey conducted by McKinsey wherein 64% and 83% of all firms fall short of the planned cost and reve-nue synergies respectively (Christofferson, McNish and Sias 2004; Early 2004). It therefore appears that an overly optimistic estimation of the synergistic potential is a major reason for the failure of many M&A (Kode, Ford and Sutherland 2003, p. 27). Due to its relevance for M&A, it is deemed necessary to discuss the concept and effectiveness of synergy in more detail in the following pages.

2.2.1 Acquisition premium and synergistic potential

Before making an acquisition, the acquiring firm will estimate the value of the target company. A rationale buyer will only purchase a specific firm if the discounted value of the expected future income stream of the target is greater than the purchase price consideration. In turn, the shareholders of the target company will not sell their shares unless the offer price exceeds the discounted value of the expected future income stream. The valuation of a firm is subjective due to the uncertainty with re-

spect to the prediction of future events and largely depends on the extent and reliability of the information at hand at the time of the appraisal. The value of a target
firm can be expressed in a single value or as a value range (Bertoncel 2006, p. 117).

There are three different definitions of firm value, namely i) intrinsic value, ii) market
value and iii) synergy value (see figure 2-2). The intrinsic value states the value of
the expected future cash flows of the firm independent of any change in control,
discounted at an appropriate discount rate. The intrinsic value is also referred to as
real or true value. The market value reflects the market participant's valuation of the
firm. It includes a market premium in anticipation of a potential takeover. In the case
of a stock listed company, the market value is equivalent to the market capitalization,
i.e. the number of shares multiplied by the share price. The synergy value comprises
the present value of cash flows that are derived from improvements in the combined
entity beyond the stand-alone values of the individual firms (Eccles, Lanes and
Wilson 1999, p. 140). The acquisition price refers to a final negotiated purchase price
consideration for the target company. The excess amount of the purchase price over
the market value is referred to as an acquisition premium. It represents an allocation
of future benefit to the shareholders of the target company. Hence, the acquirer
needs to determine the synergy value of the target company and the portion to be
shared with the shareholders of the acquisition target (Bertoncel 2006, p. 118).

Many acquisitions fail to create shareholder value for the buyer due to excessive
premiums paid in relation to the potential synergies which could be achieved from a
merger. Since the synergy value represents the maximum premium that a buyer can
afford to pay over the market value of the target company, it is of utmost importance
to the acquirer to obtain a comprehensive understanding of the potential synergies
(Kode et al. 2003, p. 27). In this context, it could be reasoned that there is a direct
relationship between the size of the acquisition premium and the value of the antici-
pated synergies (Kode et al. 2003, p. 30). This notion is however challenged by
Sirower's *synergy limitation view* which posits a low correlation between the premium
and the potential for efficiency gains. His argument is based on the assumption that
there are severe limits to the improvements that the acquiring firm's management
can generally achieve through acquisitions. He therefore argues that the premium
provides an up-front indication of the risk of an acquisition failure (Sirower 1997, p.

89). His study of a sample of 168 acquisitions effected during the period 1979 through 1990 reveals a high negative correlation between the acquisition premium and the post-merger performance of the acquiring firm (Sirower 1997, p. 167).

Figure 2-2: Basic principle of target valuation

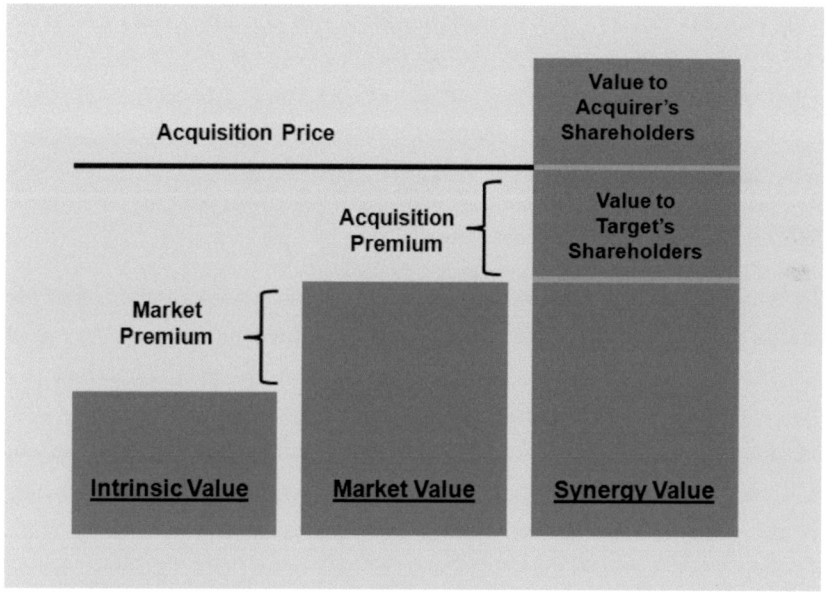

Source: Adapted from Eccles et al. 1999, p. 140

The significance of the synergy valuation is underpinned by the fact that the acquisition premium is paid up-front, while the corresponding synergies only occur progressively in the future. Hence, future gains need to be valued at their discounted present value when compared to the acquisition premium. Furthermore, the risk and probability of achieving the envisaged synergies is to be considered (Kode et al. 2003, p. 29).

2.2.2 The concept of synergy

The etymology of the term synergy derives from the Greece prefix "syn" and the verb "ergein". Thus, synergy (Greek "synergon") can be translated as "working together" (Hofmann 2005, p. 483).

In the business literature, the expression synergy was first introduced by Ansoff in 1965 in his book *Corporate Strategy*. Two decades later, the discussion about synergistic effects was taken up again and revived by Porter in *Competitive Advantage* in 1985. The above-mentioned contributions, which have made a significant impact on the discussion about synergistic effects, are introduced here.

2.2.2.1   The synergy concept of Ansoff

The concept of synergy has been defined by Ansoff as joint effects resulting from the addition of new product/markets (1965, p. 28). The starting point of Ansoff's train of thought is the return on investment (ROI) which describes the firm's annual return as a function of sales, operating cost and investment. The author argues that an integrated firm can realize scale effects leading to a lower level of operating cost and investment as compared to a firm with independent operating units while maintaining the same level of sales. Hence, synergy creates a combined return on the firm's resources which is greater than the sum of its independent parts. This phenomenon is often referred to as the "2+2=5-effect" (Ansoff 1965, p. 75).

Based on the ROI formula, Ansoff distinguishes between three synergy types, namely sales, operating and investment synergy. Sales synergy can occur as a result of the common use of distribution channels, sales administration and warehousing as well as shared marketing activities for a complete range of related products. Operating synergy results from the increased utilization of labour and production factors, learning curve advantages and bulk purchasing, while investment synergy can be achieved from the joint utilization of machinery, raw materials and the transfer of research and development intelligence. In addition, although not directly apparent from the ROI formula, Ansoff introduces management synergy as a fourth synergy type which denotes the capability of the management to apply their capabilities and knowledge in a new industry (1965, p. 75). Based on the successive phases of a new product/market activity, Ansoff differentiates between start-up synergy and operating synergy. Start-up synergy resembles one-off effects, while operating synergy describes on-going synergistic effects from a going concern (Ansoff 1966, cited in: Hofmann 2004, p. 241).

Ansoff furthermore introduces a framework for the evaluation of synergy. He suggests capturing synergy based on the functional areas of the firm, i.e. general management and finance, research and development, marketing and manufacturing. Subsequently, a competence profile is established by rating the firm's skills and resources with respect to other companies. Ansoff suggests considering four categories of skills and resources, namely i) facilities and equipment, ii) personnel skills, iii) organizational capabilities and iv) management capabilities. Synergistic opportunities are eventually unveiled by comparing the competence profile with competitive profiles of selected industries (Ansoff 1965, pp. 81-93). Ansoff furthermore links the concept of synergy directly to the choice of strategy. "A natural companion to the competitive advantage is the synergy component of strategy. This requires that opportunities within the scope possess characteristics which will enhance synergy" (Ansoff 1965, p. 165). Moreover, he stresses the importance of timing advantages during the start-up phase, especially in dynamic environments (Ansoff 1965, p. 79).

As is apparent from the discussion on functional synergy between industry groups, Ansoff expects a higher synergy potential for related industries, while a lesser amount is projected for diversification from an existing industry into another unrelated industry. In this context, the author acknowledges the possibility of negative synergy which may occur from the diversification into a new industry (Ansoff 1965, pp. 76-77). Negative synergy is often described as dyssynergy or "2+2=3" effect (Hofmann 2005, p. 484). His stance, that synergy is more likely to occur in related M&A, is also apparent from his discussion on diversification. He argues that firms may decide to diversify "when synergy is not an important consideration and hence synergy advantages of expansion over diversification are not important" (Ansoff 1965, p. 114). Ansoff furthermore stresses that synergy merely describes potential effects which need to be captured through appropriate integration of the new venture into the parent organization which demands the matching of the resources and skills to the requirements of the new product/market area (Ansoff 1965, pp. 77-78).

In summary, Ansoff provides an important contribution with regards to the concept of synergy. He introduces a classification of synergy types and links synergy to corporate strategy and diversification. His classification of different synergy effects however lacks clarity. He identifies three synergy types, namely sales, operating and investment synergy following the ROI formula, and introduces management synergy as a fourth synergy type. Yet, in his discussion on the framework for the evaluation of synergy he suggests that "a fourth synergistic effect is acceleration of the respective changes in the three variables" sales, operating and investment synergy (Ansoff 1965, p. 81). His analysis does not provide an explanation on the underlying mechanisms which are the cause of synergy creation (Hofmann 2004, p. 241).

2.2.2.2   The synergy concept of Porter

In contrast to Ansoff, who views synergy in the context of new product/market ventures, Porter takes a critical stance on corporate strategy and the notion to create value through diversification. Porter supports his argument with findings from a review of the M&A activity of 33 U.S. conglomerates, which revealed that 60% of acquisitions in new fields were later divested. The author explains that competitive advantage is created in the business units, while corporate strategy targeted at a diversified portfolio often results in constraints for the business and additional overhead expenses (Porter 1987, p. 46).

Hence, Porter considers synergy in the context of business strategy, specifically horizontal strategy which addresses policies and objectives across interrelated business units within the firm's existing portfolio. Referring to the large number of diversification-based M&A in the 1960s and 1970s which have largely been motivated by the realization of synergy, Porter does not see the failure to achieve the expected value gains in fundamental flaws of the concept, but in a poor understanding of synergy as well as a lack of appropriate tools and improper implementation. "Ill-defined notions of what constituted synergy underlay many companies' acquisition strategies" (Porter 1985, p. 318).

Figure 2-3: The generic value chain

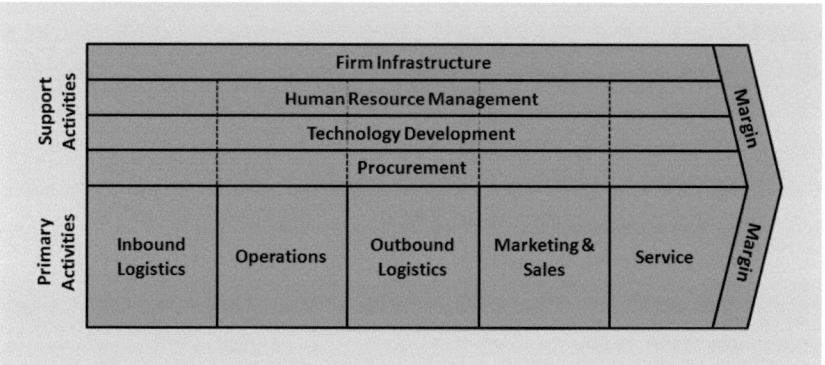

Source: Porter 1985, p. 37

Porter takes the view that synergy can be realized through the identification and exploitation of interrelationships between related business units. The author defines interrelationships as "tangible opportunities to reduce costs or enhance differentiation in virtually any activity in the value chain" (Porter 1985, p. 318). He introduces the value chain as a tool to identify and analyse synergistic opportunities. "The value chain disaggregates a firm into its strategically relevant activities in order to understand the behaviour of costs and the existing and potential source of differentiation" (Porter 1985, p. 33). Porter identifies nine generic activities which are classified into primary and support activities. Each primary and support activity contributes to the creation of competitive advantage either through direct value activities, indirect value activities or quality assurance activities (Porter 1985, p. 43) (see figure 2-3).

Moreover, the author distinguishes between three categories of interrelationships, namely i) tangible interrelationships, ii) intangible interrelationships and iii) competitor interrelationships (Porter 1985, p. 323-5). Tangible interrelationships are described as sharing of activities between business units, such as joint procurement or joint sales and marketing. Implementing tangible interrelationships, which requires common buyers, production processes, technologies or channels, results in competitive advantage if lower cost or enhanced differentiation from sharing of activities exceeds the cost of sharing (Porter 1985, p. 324). Intangible interrelationships are depicted as the transfer of management skills and knowledge among separate value chains. Value is created if the improvement in cost or differentiation exceeds the cost of transferring know-how between business units (Porter 1985, p. 350). Competitor interrelationships resemble a specific competitive situation in which two rival firms compete in more than one industry. They may exist without tangible or intangible interrelationships being present (Porter 1985, p. 325). Thus, competitive interrelationships apparently do not constitute a distinct source of synergy, but merely underpin the importance of tangible and intangible interrelationships due to the fact that actions in one industry may have implications in another industry (Rodermann 1999, p. 50).

Porter stresses the relevance of the cost of sharing. He differentiates between i) cost of coordination, ii) cost of compromise and iii) cost of inflexibility. The cost of coordination constitutes the additional effort of the business units to resolve problems related to the sharing of value chain activities which may require additional management attention as well as cost in terms of personnel and financial resources (Porter 1985, p. 331). The cost of compromise relates to the fact that the sharing business units might need to deviate from the optimal process in an isolated operation, while the cost of inflexibility may take effect in the form of deferred reaction to competitor moves, as well as exit barriers as a result of interdependencies with other business units (Porter 1985, p. 333). The cost of sharing can result in decreasing profitability levels. This indicates that negative synergy can arise from the joint use of resources as already observed by Ansoff (1965, p. 76).

Ansoff's concept of synergy has been advanced by Porter who differentiates between tangible and intangible synergies and introduces the value chain as a tool to identify and analyse synergistic potentials (Rodermann 1999, p. 51). It however remains unclear why Porter considers competitor interrelationships in his discussion on synergy since the author himself points out that competitor interrelationships are not to be considered a distinct source of synergy. In summary, it can be stated that both authors do not offer an explicit definition of synergy and a comprehensive explanation of the underlying mechanism (Hofmann 2004, p. 244). Therefore, the more recent literature on the concept of synergy and its effectiveness shall be reviewed. The researcher will furthermore provide a classification of synergy types.

2.2.3 Synergy types and effectiveness

It is argued by Chatterjee that an acquisition strategy will yield economic value, if a scarce resource is matched to an opportunity. He refers to the resource-based view of the firm (Wernerfelt 1984), which relates the amount of economic value that can be achieved in M&A to i) the amount of resources held by the firm in relation to the total amount of resources available in the market and ii) the availability of opportunities to put the relevant resource to work (Chatterjee 1986, p. 121). Hence, synergy can be defined as "increased value [which] results from an opportunity to utilize a specialized resource which arises solely as a result of the merger" (Jensen and Ruback 1983, in: Chatterjee 1986, p. 119).

Two major synergy types shall be distinguished for the purpose of this study, namely i) income synergy and ii) cost synergy. This classification appears appropriate since synergistic effects eventually translate into revenue enhancements or cost reductions. Accordingly, all synergistic potentials are typically quantified in terms of income and cost during the pre-merger evaluation of an acquisition target (Lechner and Meyer 2003, p. 312). Beneficial effects which do not increase the efficiency of the firm, such as reduced risk or increased market power, are usually not related to the concept of synergy (Rodermann 1999, p. 38).

The extant literature sometimes suggests financial and collusive synergy as distinct synergy types (Chatterjee 1986; Trautwein 1990). Financial synergy leads to a reduction in the cost of capital, while collusive synergy results in value gains as a result of market power (Chatterjee 1986, p. 121). The idea of financial synergy can be criticized for its theoretical foundation since it implies privileged access to capital for some firms which is however not possible in efficient capital markets (Trautwein 1990, p. 284). The concept of collusive synergy is based on a re-distribution of wealth between the market participants and does not create additional economic value (Rodermann 1999). It is furthermore important to note that anti-trust regulations put limitations on the ability of the market participants to achieve collusive synergy (Wildemann 2003, p. 598). Hence, only operational synergy will be considered in this study in line with the efficiency theory, while financial and collusive synergies are excluded from the scope of the research project.

In addition to positive synergistic effects, the combination of two previously independent entities might also result in negative effects on the income and cost situation, which are commonly referred to as dyssynergy or negative synergy (Hofmann 2004; Hofmann 2005). Negative synergy encompasses all direct expenses related to an acquisition, such as legal costs, relocation costs and cost for the integration and harmonization of the IT infrastructure, as well as indirect expenses and detrimental effects on the income situation (Lechner and Meyer 2003, p. 315; Lechner 2007b, p. 24). In order to determine the net synergies achieved in an acquisition, the amount of dyssynergies incurred needs to be subtracted from the synergies achieved (Lechner and Meyer 2003, p. 312; Hofmann 2004, p. 285). This relationship can be illustrated in the equation:

Net synergies = Synergy – Dyssynergy

In summary, for the purpose of the study, the following synergy classification is proposed: i) cost synergy, ii) income synergy, iii) cost dyssynergy and iv) income dyssynergy. This distinction appears useful since practitioners view synergy primarily as operational effects in terms of income and cost (Chatterjee 2007, p. 46).

2.2.3.1 Cost synergy

Cost synergies constitute operational reductions in cost which are derived from the sharing of value chain activities (Hofmann 2004, p. 272). The following underlying mechanisms can be distinguished which result in cost synergies, namely i) economies of scale, ii) learning and iii) economies of scope.

Economies of scale can be realized from efficiency improvements in production at a higher scale, or from a less than proportional increment in the infrastructure and overhead costs needed to support the operation with increasing production volume (Porter 1985, p. 71). More specifically, the effect of economies of scale is based on the fact that fixed costs of production remain constant despite an increasing production volume. As a result the cost per unit is decreasing with a higher production volume since the fixed costs can be allocated to a larger number of units (Hofmann 2004, p. 274). In this context it is important to note that the scale sensitivity of different value chain activities varies significantly. Product development is typically more scale sensitive than sales force operation since the cost of this value chain activity is "heavily fixed no matter what the firm's scale is" (Porter 1985, p. 71). Cost reduction achieved from increased capacity utilization needs to clearly distinguished from economies of scale. Increasing capacity utilization allows spreading the fixed costs for existing personnel and production facilities over a larger volume, while economies of scale imply that a production at full capacity is more efficient at a larger scale (Porter 1985, p. 71). Whenever a value chain activity has a high proportion of fixed costs, it is especially vulnerable for underutilization. In this respect, fixed cost will create a penalty for underutilization of capacity (Porter 1985, p. 74).

The cost to perform a value chain activity can decline over time due to learning which increases its overall efficiency. This phenomenon is described as the *learning curve effect* which states that labour costs per unit will decrease with increasing production output (Yelle 1974). The learning curve effect is often used interchangeably with the term *experience curve effect*. The learning curve effect however focuses primarily on efficiency gains in the area of labour cost due to short-term learning-by-doing, while the experience curve effect considers the total cost of production in various areas over the entire life of a product (Hall and Howell 1985, p. 197). The underlying driver of the learning and experience curve effects is primarily the accumulated production output. It can therefore be argued that the learning and experience curve effects merely resemble economies of scale. In fact, learning from sharing of value chain activities is largely scale sensitive. On the other hand, transferring skills between business units may result in scale independent learning effects (Porter 1985, p. 328). In line with Porter, cost synergies from learning shall therefore "encompass all types of cost reduction that result from improving know-how and procedures independent of scale" (Porter 1985, p. 73).

Cost synergies may furthermore arise from economies of scope which are relevant to multi-product companies. Economies of scope arise whenever it is less costly to combine the production of two or more products in one firm than the production in two separate companies. The cost savings originate from the sharing of the same input factor for more than one product without complete congestion (Panzar and Willig 1981, p. 268). Economies of scope are therefore linked to the product range while economies of scale are a function of the production volume (Wöginger 2004, p. 61). An important prerequisite for economies of scope is that the relevant input factors can be applied in more than one production process without being consumed. Intangible assets, such as a patent, are typically not consumed during the production process and render themselves eligible for a simultaneous application in a multi-product scenario. As for tangible assets which are consumed during production, the available economies decline with increased capacity utilization due to competition (Jansen 2001, cited in: Wildemann 2003, p. 597).

2.2.3.2   Income synergy

Income synergy accrues from value chain linkages which allow joined activities between the previously independent entities. Hofmann distinguishes between effects that result from differentiation on the one hand and economies of scope of the other hand (2004, p. 279).

In relation to the former mechanism, the author argues that differentiation of the product offering results in increased value as perceived by the customer which allows the firm to realize price increments. Differentiation of the product offering can be achieved through the addition of product variants (horizontal differentiation), enhancing the product quality (vertical differentiation) as well as innovation (lateral differentiation). With respect to income synergy from economies of scope, Hofmann elaborates that a shared utilization of resources may likewise yield benefits from differentiation. He specifically refers to cross-selling effects which result in an increased contribution margin which is the residue of the sales price less the cost of production (Hofmann 2004, pp. 280-281).

Hofmann's distinction between income synergy through either differentiation or economies of scope appears inconclusive. Both effects are based on increasing customer value which is achieved through differentiation and are being rewarded by the willingness of customers to pay a premium for the relevant products. Hofmann argues that economies of scope are achieved through joined utilization of resources. This prerequisite however does not sufficiently discriminate between differentiation and economies of scope, since differentiation might also require the sharing of existing resources in order to achieve higher product quality as well as innovation. Moreover, Hofmann states that differentiation results in increasing price levels, while economies of scope yield a higher contribution margin which is the residual amount of price and production cost (Hofmann 2004, p. 281). Since the cost of production is irrelevant for the discussion of income synergies, differentiation and economies of scope are obviously both tapping into the same underlying mechanism, namely increasing differentiation of the product offering.

As articulated by Porter, differentiation arises from the sharing of value chain activities. Differentiation implies that a firm seeks to be unique with regards to certain dimensions which are appreciated by customers. The firm is rewarded for its uniqueness with a premium price (Porter 1985, p. 15). According to Porter, differentiation is one of two key sources of competitive advantage besides cost advantage. In his view, differentiation is not limited to production and marketing, but may arise basically anywhere in the value chain as long as value is created for the customer. Differentiation thus enables the firm to command a higher price, sell more of the same product at a given price or realize equivalent benefits such as customer loyalty (Porter 1985, p. 120). Key drivers of differentiation encompass policy choices, such as product features and value-added services, linkages within the value chain as well as supplier and channel linkages (Porter 1985, p. 124). In his discussion about horizontal strategy, Porter argues that differentiation is most likely to occur in the context of diversification. He discriminates between market-oriented, product-oriented and technology-oriented diversification. Market-oriented diversification aims at selling new products to common buyers, while product-oriented diversification targets the production of similar products with shared production facilities. Technology-oriented diversification seeks to develop new industries based on similar core technologies for new or existing customers (Porter 1985, p. 377).

In the context of M&A, cross-selling of the existing product offering of either of the previously independent firms to the customers of the other firm is often cited in the academic literature as an example of income synergy through differentiation (Wildemann 2003, p. 598). As highlighted by Porter, the sources of differentiation are however diverse and not limited to cross-selling alone (Porter 1985, p. 120).

2.2.3.3   Cost dyssynergy

During the post-merger phase, the management of the combined entity has to deal with negative effects which result from the integration of the previously independent entities. Dyssynergies are often inevitable for the creation of synergy, i.e. cost needs to be incurred in order to achieve the prerequisites for the sharing of value chain activities or the transfer of skills (Porter 1985, p. 331).

Hofmann differentiates between the five types of cost dyssynergies, namely i) coordination-related cost dyssynergies, ii) compromise-related cost dyssynergies, iii) inflexibility-related cost dyssynergies, iv) cultural and employee-related cost dyssynergies and v) speed-related dyssynergies (Hofmann 2004, pp. 284-293).

Coordination-related cost dyssynergy describes the cost incurred for the additional effort required to coordinate the sharing of value chain activities between the merging entities. The cost incurred for coordination increases with the complexity of the underlying activities. One-time costs as well as on-going costs for coordination are to be distinguished. Compromise-related cost dyssynergies arise whenever sharing of value chain activities results in one activity being executed in a suboptimal manner. A compromise might be required if the characteristics of the respective activities are too different to achieve a best practice solution. Inflexibility-related cost dyssynergies are caused by restrictions imposed on one business unit due to linkages with another business unit. In order to achieve the same level of flexibility, additional expenditure might be required by one business unit compared to the pre-merger situation. Besides, exit barriers may increase since the termination of one business unit might affect the success and flexibility of another business unit. Cultural and employee-related cost dyssynergies occur whenever the motivation of employees declines as a result of M&A. The detrimental effects of incompatible organizational cultures (Hofstede 1991) on the post-merger performance of the combined entity have been discussed in great depth in the academic literature (Chatterjee et al. 1992; Badrtalei and Bates 2007). The performance resulting from a merger is correlated to employee support which in turn depends on the cultural fit, especially the degree to which the employees of the target firm perceive their culture is compatible with the acquiring firm's culture. Dissimilar cultures can create a feeling of hostility which can significantly reduce the commitment and cooperation of employees with negative implications for the profitability of the combined firm (Chatterjee et al. 1992, p. 321). In order to reduce or overcome friction from cultural differences, the management of the combined entity can resort to a tool kit of different measures, such as seminars, workshops and team building events, which in turn result in incremental costs (dyssynergies). Furthermore, the M&A might result in other employee-related measures which involve additional costs, such as redundancies and special bonus payments (Hofmann 2004, p. 291).

Figure 2-4: Relationship between speed of integration and cost dyssynergy

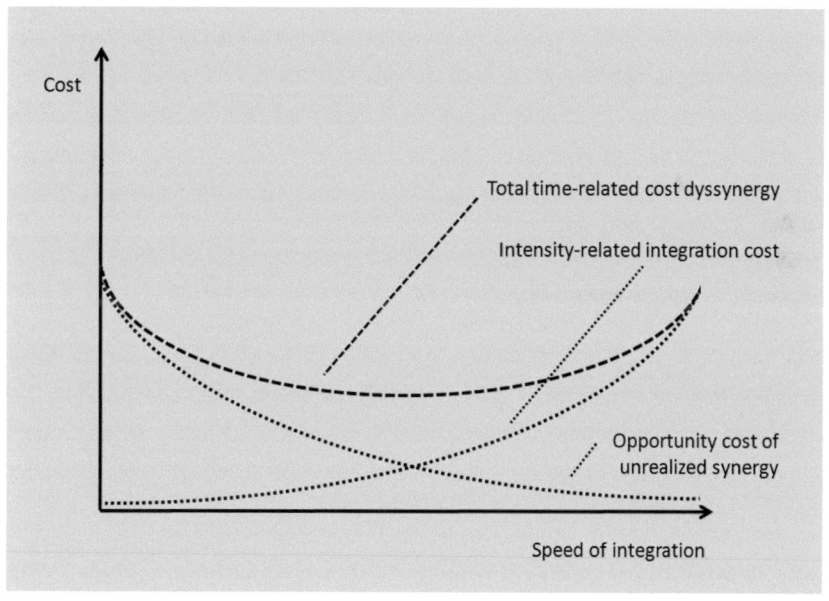

Source: Hofmann 2004, p. 290

In addition to the above mentioned effects, Hofmann introduces speed-related effects as a discretionary cost dyssynergy. He argues that the total cost of the post-merger integration can be split into the opportunity cost for missed synergies and the cost of the post-merger integration project. If the integration is executed at a high speed, the probability of capturing the planned synergies increases and the opportunity cost for missed synergistic potential declines accordingly. At the same time, the cost of integration is likely to increase due to a growing utilisation of scarce resources, such as management time, as well as the increasing intensity of the integration project and related detrimental effects (Hofmann 2004, p. 290). The speed of integration can therefore be translated into a cost-benefit equation which is illustrated in figure 2-4.

The speed of integration is also referred to as *economies of time* which suggest the existence of a discretionary synergistic effect (Hofmann 2004, p. 289). A specific mechanism for economies of time which is different to the other synergistic effects can not be identified. Instead it appears that decisions with regard to the chronological sequence of integration related measures constitutes a trade off between certain synergistic effects, specifically the synergy realization on the one hand and the cost of integration on the other hand. Therefore, time-related cost dyssynergies are not considered as a distinct synergistic effect in this study. Instead, the speed of integration will be considered as a moderating effect on the synergy management process (Homburg and Bucerius 2006).

2.2.3.4   Income dyssynergy

M&A may result in adverse effects on the income situation of the combined entity which are referred to as income dyssynergy. These effects might be caused by the expectations and perceptions of customers with regards to the quality of the product offering and the brand image as well as to the increased dependency of customers from the merged firm (Hofmann 2004, p. 293).

First, the integration of previously independent firms can result in uncertainty on the side of customers concerning the quality of products as well as the terms and conditions. Moreover, organizational restructuring during the post-merger integration might impair existing customer relationships due to transfer of staff or resignation of employees. These effects might result in declining sales with existing customers. The customer perception of the company image and quality of the product offering can be adversely influenced due to negative spill-over effects. This can be the case if the divergent images of similar product offerings result in a dilution of the brand image. Furthermore, it is possible that the negative image of one brand is perceived more strongly by clients than the positive image of a premium brand, leading to an overall reduction of the reputation of the brand (Hofmann 2004, pp. 293-297).

Second, customers might perceive M&A as a threat due to increasing dependency from their supplier. In order to reduce the risk of procurement and to maintain flexibility and independence, customers typically do not contract the entire demand for one input factor to a single supplier. In the case of a horizontal merger between existing suppliers, the independence of the customer might be reduced prompting him to award part of his demand to a third supplier leading to a reduction of sales of the combined entity compared to the pre-merger situation (Hofmann 2004, p. 298).

2.3   Business relatedness and M&A performance

The impact of diversification on firm performance in general, and specifically in the context of M&A, has caught the attention of researchers for many decades (Bruner 2002, p. 48). The fundamental question of the research is whether diversification strategies overall result in increasing shareholder value. A key prerequisite for research undertaken in this area is a reliable and widely accepted measure of firm diversification. Hence, the measurement concepts for the degree of diversification shall be introduced before past studies on the relationship between M&A performance and relatedness are discussed.

2.3.1 Measurement of business relatedness

The degree of diversification is often referred to as *relatedness* or *business relatedness* (Chatterjee and Wernerfelt 1991b; Stimpert and Duhaime 1997; Pehrsson 2006b; Chatterjee 2007). Past research has focused primarily on two different measures of relatedness, namely i) continuous product-count measures and ii) categorical measures based on researchers' assessments (Montgomery 1982, p. 299). A more recent stream of research has focused on managerial perceptions considering a broader range of different attributes which are relevant to determine business relatedness (Stimpert and Duhaime 1997; Pehrsson 2006a; Pehrsson 2006b).

Figure 2-5: Measurement approaches to business relatedness

Product-count Measures	Researcher Assessment	Managerial Perceptions
SIC codes • Finkelstein 1992 • Lubatkin et al. 1993 • Hall and John 1994	Product-market attributes • Wrigley 1970 • Rumelt 1974, 1982	• Nayyar 1992 • Stimpert and Duhaime 1997 • Pehrsson 2006
FTC classification • Chatterjee 1986 • Lubatkin 1987 • Singh and Montgomery 1987	Resource attributes • Montgomery 1982 • Peteraf 1993 • Harrision and Hall 1994	
	Value-chain attributes • Porter 1985 • John and Harrison 1999 • Tsai 2000	

Source: Adapted from Pehrsson 2006b, p. 353

2.3.1.1   Product-count measures

Investigations which apply the product-count measure usually draw on the Standard Industrial Classification (SIC) (Rhoades 1974; Bass, Cattin and Wittink 1978). The SIC system is a numerical catalogue of the federal government classifying all types of economic activities in the US economy. In 1997 the SIC system was replaced by the North American Industry Classification System, however certain government agencies and departments, such as the U.S. Securities and Exchange Commission (SEC), are still using the SIC codes (SEC 2009). The SIC system is based on a classification of the firm's establishments according to its primary activities. The application of product-count measures ranges from simple counts of the SIC codes to a weighted approach based on the significance of the respective activities (Montgomery 1982, pp. 299-300).

The product-count approach based on the SIC system offers the advantage of being a concrete, objective and replicable approach. Critics of the product-count approach however highlight deficiencies in the underlying SIC system, specifically the lack of guiding principles for the assignment of activities to a SIC code, such as products, market structure or the nature of raw materials. As a consequence, products which are substitutes for one another can be classified in disparate SIC codes due to differences in the manufacturing process. Conversely, if an industry is classified based on market-oriented criteria, products manufactured in radically different production processes can be assigned to the same SIC code (Montgomery 1982, p. 300). Thus, the distance between SIC codes cannot always be interpreted as an appropriate measure of the degree of relatedness between certain activities (Rumelt 1982, p. 360).

In addition to the SIC systematic, which was originally devised to describe the strategic focus of a single diversified firm, the relatedness of two merging entities can be determined based on the categorical classification of the U.S. Federal Trade Commission (FTC) (Federal Trade Commission 1981). The FTC category system groups M&A into five mutually exclusive groups, namely i) horizontal, ii) vertical, iii) product extension, iv) market extension and v) unrelated transactions. The horizontal category consists of the combination of firms which produce one or more of the same product in the same geographic market, while vertical transactions describe M&A between firms with a buyer-seller relationship. The category product extension refers to functionally related firms in terms of production and distribution which however do not compete directly with their products. Market extension, in turn, describes M&A of companies which sell the same products in different geographic markets. Unrelated M&A involves companies which do not exhibit any similarities in terms of their product/market presence (Walsh 1988, p. 174). Many studies investigating the impact of relatedness on M&A performance have applied the FTC systematic (Chatterjee 1986; Lubatkin 1987; Singh and Montgomery 1987). While the FTC approach offers a simple and readily available classification of relatedness, it suffers from the same conceptual difficulties as the SIC systematic since "both are essentially product-count measures and therefore cannot be expected to be able to identify the more complex nature of relatedness that is of the primary interest in diversification research [...]" (Lubatkin 1987, p. 41).

2.3.1.2   Researcher assessment

The criticism of the product-count approach has been addressed by the categorical measurement approach devised by Wrigley (1970) who classifies firms based on their diversification strategies. The key feature of the categorical measurement approach of Wrigley is to determine "first, the extent of the firm's involvement in activities which draw upon different skills and, second, the way in which new activities are *related* to old activities" (Grant and Jammine 1988, p. 333). Accordingly, the classification of diversification strategies is determined based on two dimensions, namely i) the specialization ratio (SR) determined as the firm's sales of its major activity in proportion of its total sales and ii) the related ratio (RR) which indicates the proportion of the firm's sales in activities which are related to one another. The Wrigley categorical classification is illustrated in figure 2-6.

Figure 2-6: Wrigley's categorical classification of diversification strategies

	SR	RR
Single Business	> 95%	N/A
Dominant Business	< 95% / > 70%	N/A
Related Business	< 70%	> 70%
Unrelated Business	< 70%	< 70%

SR = Specilization Ratio, RR = Related Ratio

Source: Adapted from Grant and Jammine 1988, p. 334

Wrigley's classification was later refined by Rumelt (1974) with the introduction of dimensions of relatedness. Rumelt classifies a firm based on nine different diversification categories depending on the sales that can be attributed to a discrete business area. Furthermore, the author differentiates constrained and linked patterns of diversification. In a constrained pattern the firm's activities are all related to one another, while in a vertical pattern each activity is only related to at least one activity, but not to all other activities. The categorical measurement approach of Rumelt offers the advantage of combining quantitative data with qualitative aspects, such as the strategic focus of the firm (Montgomery 1982, p. 302). In Rumelt's measurement system, a continuous measure is applied to assign a firm to a strategy category. The underlying distinct business areas are however determined by the researcher thus adding a subjective element to the relatedness measurement which resembles a major difference to the product-count systematic (Lubatkin 1993).

Despite this fact, Rumelt's categorical measurement approach yields results which have a high correlation to SIC based product-count measures which suggests that both measurement approaches tap into the same underlying concept (Montgomery 1982, p. 305; Lubatkin 1993, p. 447). This finding has facilitated research into firm diversification based on product-count measures since relatedness could be measured with sufficient reliability based on archival accounting data rather than laborious analysis of the firm's products, markets and technologies which are required for Rumelt's taxonomy (Stimpert and Duhaime 1997, p. 112).

While the classification of Rumelt/Wrigley focuses mainly on product/market attributes, other researchers have assessed the degree of diversification on different characteristics of the firm, such as resources (Montgomery 1982; Peteraf 1993; Harrison, Hall and Nargundkar 1993) and value chain attributes (Porter 1985; John and Harrison 1999; Tsai 2000).

2.3.1.3   Managerial perceptions

Despite the large number of research projects undertaken in the field, there is still no consistent explanation concerning the impact of relatedness on firm performance (Bruner 2004, p. 69). Lemlin argues that the lack of explanatory power can be attributed to "an inadequate conceptualization of relatedness" and stresses the relevance of other sources of relatedness, such as complementary product use, similarity of differentiation techniques and technical knowledge (Lemlin 1982, cited in: Stimpert and Duhaime 1997, p. 112). Similarly, Keats questions whether sales data by business unit is sufficient to capture the complex phenomenon of relatedness advocating "a richer conceptualization that can incorporate considerations of managerial issues and treatment of various forms of diversification as potential solutions to a multivariate set of problems" (Keats 1990, p. 69).

Based on this criticism of established measures of diversification, another stream of research explored a behavioural perspective on diversification with focus on managerial perceptions of business relatedness (Nayyar 1992; Stimpert and Duhaime 1997; Pehrsson 2006a; Pehrsson 2006b). A key rationale of the research is to shift the view from an external angle towards an internal assessment of relatedness as perceived by the firm's management. When making their assessment concerning business relatedness, managers select, interpret and discuss information while relying on their personal perceptions. The human perception can be defined as the "active process of organizing the stimulus information and giving it meaning" (May 2007, cited in: Pehrsson 2009, p. 6).

An internal view of relatedness is relevant since strategic decisions are made based on the manager's understanding and perception of business relatedness (Pehrsson 2006b, p. 355). Measures of relatedness based on managerial perceptions offer the opportunity to capture different attributes of business relatedness which is important given the complex challenges management faces in the process of diversification. "Moreover, the top managers of diversified firms must endeavour to realize synergies that justify their firm's diversification strategies" (Stimpert and Duhaime 1997, p. 113). On the other hand, managerial perceptions of relatedness might be ambiguous, idiosyncratic and hence different to the understanding of interrelationships between businesses as viewed by the researcher (Pehrsson 2006a, p. 268). "However, research evidence also suggests that different conceptualizations may be shared or even widely held among managers of different firms in the same industry" (Pehrsson 2009, p. 7).

In order to explore the conceptualization of relatedness by managers, Stimpert and Duhaime (1997) approached 915 CEOs of the 1,000 largest industrial companies in the U.S.A. (final sample 174; response rate 19%) based on a broad range of relatedness dimensions identified from the literature. Using factor analysis to reveal underlying commonalities, the researchers identified four dimensions of relatedness, namely i) product/market relatedness, ii) differentiation relatedness, iii) financial relatedness and iv) commodity relatedness. The data however suffered from cross-loading between individual items. Furthermore, the first two factors already explained about 70% of the variance, while the remaining dimensions had little explanatory power (Stimpert and Duhaime 1997, p. 120).

The idea of a multidimensional construct of business relatedness based on managerial perceptions was further refined by Pehrsson (2006a) whose study was based on a survey of 304 Swedish manufacturing firms with a final sample size of 124 completed questionnaires (response rate 41%). Based on established measures of relatedness, Pehrsson identified 16 individual variables of product/market, resource and value chain related attributes. The two main business units of the surveyed companies which most clearly resembled the core competence of the firm were compared based on the individual variables. With the help of factor analysis, the researcher identified six factors of business relatedness, namely i) product technology, ii) general management skills, iii) end customers, iv) brand recognition, v) supply channel types and vi) market knowledge.

As compared to Stimpert and Duhaime's study, the variance explained by the individual factors is more evenly distributed. The item reliability was tested using Cronbach's coefficient alpha. Except for the last factor *market knowledge*, the individual values exceeded 0.60 which is considered the minimum requirement for newly developed scales (Tharenou, Donohue and Cooper 2007, p. 153). As such, the study provides additional support for the notion that business relatedness should be viewed as a multidimensional construct. The research project furthermore suggests five important factors instead of three major attribute categories: product/markets, resources and value chains identified in previous studies (Pehrsson 2006a, p. 277).

Figure 2-7: Factors of multidimensional construct relatedness

Factor 1 Product Technology	Factor 2 General Management Skills	Factor 3 End Customers	Factor 4 Brand Recognition	Factor 5 Supply Channel Types	Factor 6 Market Knowledge
• Product Technology • Product Use • Product Design • Pricing	• General Management Skills • Technical Skills • Administrative Skills	• End Customer Types • Sales Channel Types • After Sales Services	• Brand Recognition • Brand Identity	• Supply Channel Types • Suppliers	• Market Knowledge • Competitors

Source: Adapted from Pehrsson 2006a, p. 272

2.3.2 The impact of business relatedness on M&A performance

A significant amount of research has been conducted on the key drivers that influence the performance of M&A (cf. meta-analyses of Datta et al. 1992; Bruner 2004
for an overview of past research projects). For many decades, researchers have
taken a particular interest in the concept of business relatedness (Rumelt 1982;
Chatterjee 1986; Singh and Montgomery 1987; Harrison et al. 1991; Chatterjee
2007). The research was initiated by the question whether M&A between entities
which are related in product/market or technological terms will improve the performance of M&A.

In a longitudinal study conducted by Rumelt (1982), the impact of relatedness on the
return on investment has been investigated for the largest 500 U.S. companies during the period from 1949 to 1974. The data revealed that firms which fall into the
dominant vertical and unrelated business categories showed a significantly lower
level of profitability as compared to related businesses (Rumelt 1982, p. 362). While
Rumelt's study did not specifically consider performance gains in the context of
M&A, the diversification contingency framework formulated in this research project
laid the foundation for future investigations in the field of M&A (Lubatkin 1987, p. 40).

A subsequent stream of research focused on the conditions of merger performance (cf. e.g. Kitching 1967; Lubatkin 1983; Hitt et al. 1998). Aside from cultural issues during the post-merger integration, a key area of interest was the impact of strategic fit in M&A which describes the extent of unifying features between the merging entities (Chatterjee et al. 1992, p. 319). The underlying idea of the research is that a good strategic fit between the acquirer and the target company will increase the performance gains to the acquired firm. The concept of synergy, which occurs through appropriate allocation of skills and resources, provides the basis for this understanding (Lubatkin 1983, p. 218). In the context of conglomerate mergers, the notion of strategic fit therefore suggests "that a diversifier should seek merger partners which can either make use of a skill it possess ('supplementary diversification') or supply a skill it lacks ('complementary diversification')" (Pitts 1980, p. 293). The degree of strategic fit between the merging entities has been established in the relevant research through different measures of business relatedness, most commonly through SIC codes or the FTC classification.

2.3.3 Findings of past research projects

In the following section, the findings of past research projects in the subject area shall be reviewed. First, studies investigating the performance effects of M&A using product/market attributes based on SIC and FTC classifications shall be discussed. Second, a more recent stream of research shall be introduced which considers to what extent the relatedness of resource attributes impacts M&A performance.

2.3.3.1   Research projects based on product/market attributes

In Kitching's (1967) study the executives of 22 firms were interviewed. A total number of 69 acquisitions conducted by the companies during the period 1960-1965 were considered in the sample. Using the FTC classification, the author focused on the extent to which synergy could be realized in different functions. Based on the common notion at the time, the author expected synergy to be highest in the area of production due the possible realization of economies of scale as well as to increase the purchasing power and the efficiency of machinery (Kitching 1967, p. 92). The research findings however revealed that synergies in production are rated to be the area with the least dollar payoffs from synergy after acquisitions while financial and marketing synergies scored highest. The author argues that the limited possibility of capturing production synergies is related to the fact that most fixed costs often turn out to be volume variable therefore putting severe constraints on the possibility of realizing economies of scale (Kitching 1967, p. 94). The investigation furthermore revealed that the merger type was not a determining factor for the success of M&A (Kitching 1967, p. 92).

Lubatkin (1983) reviewed major research projects on mergers and the performance of the acquiring firms during 1971-1980. The findings of the meta-analysis suggest that synergistic benefits are highest in horizontal / product concentric and market concentric M&A due to the possibility of exploiting technical economies, especially in the area of production and marketing, as well as from experience curve effects (Lubatkin 1983, p. 220). The author argues that the contradictory findings to Kitching's study might be attributed to the focus on technological economies and methodological weaknesses in the latter's research project, such as the small sample of only 22 executives as well as the use of practitioner's opinion as opposed to actual performance data (Lubatkin 1983, p. 223).

In Chatterjee's (1986) study, the performance gains of merging firms for a sample of 157 mergers during the period from 1969 to 1972 was investigated using data from FTC's *Statistical Report of Mergers and Acquisitions*. The results of the study revealed higher wealth gains for the acquirer in unrelated mergers as opposed to related, non-horizontal mergers. The author speculates that this finding might be related to the higher bargaining power of acquiring companies which pursue financial synergies in unrelated acquisitions. Chatterjee argues that an acquirer with a relatively cheap source of capital can pursue a larger number of alternative targets which do not need to exhibit complementarities and thus claim a higher share of the total wealth gains while the possibility of realizing operating synergies in related M&A is typically limited to only a few suitable target companies (Chatterjee 1986, p. 134). The author however concedes that the results for the acquiring firms are not strongly statistically significant which might be attributed to the larger size of the average acquiring firm compared to the size of the target companies (Chatterjee 1986, p.

133). Furthermore, it must be pointed out that Chatterjee excluded horizontal M&A in his study. The research results might have provided different results if horizontal transactions had been included in the study (Chatterjee 1986, p. 123).

In the research project conducted by Singh and Montgomery (1987) a total number of 105 acquisitions during the period 1975-1980 were analyzed with regards to the performance gains of the acquiring and acquired firms. The sample was classified into related and unrelated acquisitions using the approach of Salter and Weinhold (1979). Accordingly, M&A which revealed similarities in terms of production technologies, science-based research or products / markets were categorized as related transactions. The results showed significantly higher performance gains in related as opposed to unrelated acquisitions (Singh and Montgomery 1987, p. 384). The authors explain their results with operating synergies, i.e. i) economies of scale through expanded production of one product, ii) economies of scope through the utilization of a specific resource for the joint production of several products or iii) market power economies, which can only be realized in related acquisitions, while the performance gains in unrelated acquisitions are limited to financial synergies. Since financial synergies are also achievable in related M&A, higher performance gains typically accrue to related M&A which in addition to financial synergy also offer the opportunity to realize operating synergies (Singh and Montgomery 1987, p. 380). It must however, be pointed out that the findings of the research project only relate to the performance gains of the target firm while a statistically significant difference could not be observed for the acquiring firms (Singh and Montgomery 1987, p. 384). An investigation completed by Lubatkin (1987) on merger strategies and stockholder value could not confirm the findings of Singh and Montgomery. Based on a large sample of mergers during 1948-1979, the author investigated the impact of relatedness on M&A performance using the FTC classification. The findings confirm wealth gains for acquiring and acquired firm's stockholders, "but they do not support the popular prescription: 'All things being equal, some product and market relatedness is better than none'" (Lubatkin 1987, p. 39). The author concedes that the research findings are subject to severe limitations, such as the relative size of the merging entities which has not been sufficiently controlled in the research design (Lubatkin 1987, p. 50).

In his research project on 104 tender offers during 1962 and 1979, Seth (1990) observed higher returns for related M&A, namely horizontal, product and market extension M&A following the FTC classification, as opposed to vertical and unrelated transactions. After elimination of target firms with a market value below 10 percent of the market value of the acquiring company, the value gains and synergy scores for all subsamples increased as compared to the initial analysis including small target firms, most notably however for the category of related M&A. The author argues that this finding suggests a significant size effect in M&A which implies that substantial synergistic gains demand a target company of material size in relation to the size of the acquiring company (Seth 1990, p. 108). Seth therefore concludes that synergistic gains in large related acquisitions are greater than in large unrelated acquisitions, while no general difference can be observed in the performance gains of related versus unrelated acquisitions (Seth 1990, p. 112).

Sirower (1997) studied the conditions of M&A performance on a sample of 168 acquisitions effected during 1979 to 1990. According to the author, the success of an acquisition can be measured in terms of the net present value of the acquisition premium and the realized synergies as follows:

Net Present Value = Synergy – Acquisition Premium (Sirower 1997, p. 89).

Based on the *synergy limitation view*, Sirower expects a low correlation between the acquisition premium and the synergistic potential to the effect that "the level of the premium provides an indication of the degree of up-front (ex-ante) risk of acquisition failure" (Sirower 1997, p. 89). The data in fact confirmed a significant negative correlation between the acquisition premium and M&A performance (Sirower 1997, p. 167). With regards to the effectiveness of relatedness, Sirower does not predict a direct relationship between relatedness on the one hand and the synergistic potential and M&A performance on the other hand. Instead, he foresees a positive moderating effect of relatedness on the acquisition premium. The author argues that the adverse effect of the acquisition premium on M&A performance will be compounded for unrelated transactions since more resources are diverted away from the existing business and thus reduce the chance to achieve the ambitious performance improvements required by the high acquisition premium (Sirower 1997, p. 91). The results of the data analysis confirm Sirower's hypothesis that strategic relatedness has no direct effect on M&A performance, while weak support has been found for the moderating effect of relatedness on the acquisition premium (Sirower 1997, p. 167). Concerning the findings of earlier studies, Sirower argues that the inconclusive evidence on the impact of relatedness on M&A performance is partly attributed to measurement problems. The author elaborates that past research projects have typically captured relatedness as a dichotomous (0,1) variable and therefore given little consideration for the degree of relatedness. In his own research project, Sirower therefore measured relatedness has a continuous index with values between 0 to 1 using SIC codes (Sirower 1997, p. 107).

2.3.3.2   Research projects based on resource attributes

Another stream of research, which has applied the resource-based view of the firm, investigates the impact of differences in the resource configurations between acquiring and target companies on M&A performance. The resource-based view is closely linked to the traditional understanding of relatedness based on product attributes. In fact, as highlighted by Wernerfelt, "resources and products are two sides of the same coin" (Wernerfelt 1984, p. 171). Resources are tangible and intangible assets including capabilities and knowledge controlled by a firm to implement strategies which improve its efficiency and effectiveness (Daft 1983, cited in: Barney 1991, p. 101).

Harrison et al. (1991) found that synergy is more likely to occur as a result of differences in the resource patterns of the merging firms. It is argued that "different but complementary resource flows may be more likely to create unique and private synergy than similar resource flows" (Harrison et al. 1991, p. 187). Unique synergy refers to value gains which are not generic in nature and can only be captured by two specific firms coming together, while private means information only available to the acquiring company (Harrison et al. 1991, p. 174).

The finding of Harrison et al. is corroborated by Hitt et al. (1998) who showed that successful acquisitions were mainly based on complementary resources between the merging entities. Hitt et al. found that resource complementarities are of much greater importance for the creation of synergy than product/market relatedness. They argue that strengths in assets and resources of one firm can be transferred to the other entity leading to synergy and sustainable competitive advantages. Hitt et al. furthermore stress that "relatedness of products/markets does not necessarily imply that the two firms have complementary resources" (1998, p. 107).

However, a study conducted by Ramaswamy (1997) on the performance impact of strategic similarities in horizontal M&A in the U.S. banking industry revealed evidence contradicting the findings of Harrison and colleagues. Differences on important strategic elements, such as customer mix and marketing emphasis, were found to have a significant detrimental effect on post-merger performance. Ramaswamy acknowledges that this divergent finding might be attributed to the particularities of the banking sector. The highly regulated environment of the industry sets limits to the possibility of an auction and therefore reduces the necessity to pursue private synergy. More importantly, Harrison et al. considered related and unrelated M&A while Ramaswamy's study is confined to horizontal transactions. Due to the differences in the product/market presence evident in the sample investigated by Harrison et al., dissimilarities in the resource patterns may in fact be beneficial for the realization of synergies while being detrimental in horizontal M&A (Ramaswamy 1997, p. 712).

Larsson and Finkelstein (1999) argue in line with Harrison et al. and Hitt et al. that complementarities constitute a key success factor for synergy in M&A. In their case survey, they investigated the degree of synergy realization across a sample of 61 M&A. The key variable examined in the research project is the *combination potential* which is conceptualized as the degree of similarities and complementarities of marketing and production operation between the merging entities. Larsson and Finkelstein argue that synergy can be achieved not only through similarities but also complementarities. The data supported their hypothesis that synergy is created not only through "economies of sameness" but also through "economies of fitness" (Larsson and Finkelstein 1999, p. 15).

In a more recent study, Swaminathan, Murshed and Hulland (2008) further advanced the knowledge in the subject field. Based on a final sample of 97 U.S. stocklisted firms, the researchers investigated the impact of similarities and differences concerning the resource configuration between acquiring and target firms on post-merger performance using abnormal stock returns. Swaminathan et al. (2008) found that similar resource patterns are more favourable in M&A with the objective of consolidation, while dissimilar resources are more beneficial in conglomerate M&A. It is argued that consolidation-based M&A which primarily target cost synergies, require the combination of similar resources. In turn, dissimilar resource configurations increase value gains in diversification-based M&A which typically target an alternative use for existing resources (Swaminathan et al. 2008, p. 38).

2.3.4 Summary and discussion

In summary, it can be noted that past research projects provide conflicting evidence on the impact of relatedness on M&A performance (see figure 2-1). This might be partly attributed to the fact that the degree of relatedness was not considered. In fact, most studies have measured relatedness as a dichotomous variable based on SIC codes or the categorical FTC classification (Sirower 1997, p. 90). Furthermore, the majority of past studies focused on similarities and differences, while neglecting that different yet complementary resource or product/market patterns may also offer the potential for value creation. Recent research suggests that the right fit of similar and/or complementary resource and product/market attributes is more relevant for synergy creation in M&A (Hitt et al. 1998; Larsson and Finkelstein 1999; Swaminathan et al. 2008).

The inconsistent findings of past studies might also be related to an inadequate conceptualization of the underlying construct. Stimpert and Duhaime (1997) argue that traditional measures of business relatedness fail to capture the complex effectiveness of synergy and insufficiently reflect the challenges of diversification. Therefore, the authors devised a multi-dimensional construct of relatedness based on managerial perceptions. The four-factor approach proposed in their study however suffers from cross-loadings and the weak explanatory power of two factors.

Table 2-1: Research findings on relatedness and M&A performance

Author(s)	Dependent Variable	Independent Variable	Definition of Similarity / Relatedness	Method & Final sample size	Key Finding(s)
Kitching (1967)	Synergy was measured through extent of dollar gains and ease of achievement; M&A success / failure	Relatedness	FTC classification; mergers were classified into horizontal, vertical integration, concentric marketing, concentric technology and conglomerate	Survey of literature; interview of executives of 22 firms reviewing 69 mergers	Synergy is most difficult to achieve in the area of technology and production; merger type is not the determining factor for M&A success; negative impact of size mismatch was observed
Lubatkin (1983)	Technical economies, pecuniary ecnomies, diversification economies	Relatedness	FTC classification; mergers were classified into horizontal / product concentric, horizontal / market concentric, vertical and conglomerate	Meta-analysis of 10 merger studies during 1971-1980	Synergy is highest in horizontal / product concentric and horizontal / market concentric mergers
Chatterjee (1986)	Stockholder gains (average cumulative abnormal returns)	Relatedness	FTC classification; mergers were classified into related / non-horizontal and unrelated transactions; horizontal mergers were excluded from the study	Event study; 157 mergers during 1969-1972	Higher wealth gains for acquiring and target firms in the unrelated category
Lubatkin (1987)	Stockholder gains (cumulative abnormal returns)	Relatedness	FTC classification; mergers were classified into horizontal / product concentric, horizontal / market concentric, vertical and conglomerate	Event study; 257 acquiring firms involved in 315 large mergers; 340 acquired firms	No significant impact of product-/market relatedness on M&A performance was observed
Singh and Montgomery (1987)	Total dollar gains accruing from the merger, cumulative portfolio abnormal returns	Relatedness	Similarity is defined as the presence (versus absence) of technological or product-market relationships between acquirer and target	Event study; 105 mergers announced in the 1975-1980 period	Greater dollar gains found when the merging firms are related (versus unrelated)
Seth (1990)	Synergy gain score; stockholder gains (average cumulative abnormal returns)	Relatedness	FTC classification; merger were grouped into related (horizontal, vertical, product extension, market extension) and unrelated transactions	Event study; 104 tender offers during the period 1962 and 1979	Synergistic gains are greater in large related than in large unrelated mergers; no general difference between related vs. unrelated transactions; significant size effect observed

Author(s)	Dependent Variable	Independent Variable	Definition of Similarity / Relatedness	Method & Final sample size	Key Finding(s)
Harrison et al. (1991)	Return on assets	Similarity in administration, capital, debt and R&D	Complementarity is defined as the differences between acquirer and target concerning administration, capital, debt and R&D	Event study, regression analysis, sample size ranged from 198 to 441 mergers for different types of complementarities tested	Significant gains from differences (complementarities) between resources
Datta et al. (1992)	Shareholder wealth creation (prediction errors)	Relatedness	Conglomerate; non-conglomerate	Meta-analysis of 41 studies conducted during 1977-1989; replication analysis using multiple regression	Non-conglomerate mergers have a significant positive impact on shareholder wealth creation
Ramaswamy (1997)	Return on assets	Similarity between acquirers and targets on five strategic variables (i.e. market coverage, operational efficiency, marketing activity, client mix and risk propensity)	A distance metric was used to compute the difference between acquirers and targets on each of the five strategic variables	Event study, regression analysis, sample of 46 horizontal mergers in the banking industry	Differences had a large negative impact on performance in horizontal mergers
Sirower (1997)	Stockholder gains (average cumulative abnormal returns)	Relatedness	SIC codes; traditional dichotomous method and indexed relatedness scores	Event study; 168 mergers during 1979-1990	No main effect of relatedness on M&A performance
Hitt et al. (1998)	Return on assets	Complementarity	Complementarities concerning assets and/or resources	Case study involving 24 mergers	Complementarities explained success, even for unrelated mergers
Larsson and Finkelstein (1999)	Synergy Realization	Combination potential, organizational integration, employee resistance	Similarity of product markets and production operations versus complementary (or dissimilarity) of product markets	Survey of 61 case studies (case survey method)	Complementary operations boosted synergy realization, particularly when organizational integration was present
Swaminathan et al. (2008)	Stockholder gains (cumulative abnormal returns)	Strategic emphasis alignment; merger motive	Strategic alignment was measured as the similarity of R&D and marketing resources; consolidation and diversification mergers were distinguished	Event study; 97 mergers during 1990-2001	High strategic emphasis alignment (high relatedness) is benefical for consolidation-based mergers; low relatedness is favourable for diversification

Source: Adapted and extended from Swaminathan et al. 2008, p. 34

The measurement of business relatedness using managerial perceptions was further enhanced by Pehrsson (2006a) who developed by five-factor approach combining attributes of previous studies based research assessments, namely i) product/market, ii) resource and iii) value chain attributes. Pehrsson revealed that the construct of business relatedness in fact consists of five distinct factors, namely i) product technology, ii) general management skills, iii) end customers, iv) brand recognition and v) supply channel types.

2.4   Gap in contemporary research

The state of the academic discussion on relatedness is summarized in Bruner's (2004, p. 69) meta-analysis as follows:

> *In general, the research studies are mixed on whether strategic relatedness explains returns to buyers; eight studies find that relatedness is a significant factor in returns to buyers; four studies find no significance. Looking at the research in this area, it seems reasonable to conclude that the degree of relatedness does matter, though perhaps in ways more complicated than even a variety of studies can capture.*

The inconclusive evidence might be caused by weaknesses in the underlying measurement approach. Most studies have captured relatedness using only few attributes, most notably product/market attributes. The degree of relatedness is thereby often not taken into consideration; that is, relatedness is frequently measured as a dichotomous variable (Sirower 1997, p. 90).

In fact, as proposed by Pehrsson (2006a), it appears more appropriate to conceptualize business relatedness as a multi-dimensional construct. The proposed research project shall address this criticism and elicit the impact of business relatedness on the creation of synergy in M&A as a multi-faceted construct. As opposed to earlier research projects which have investigated the impact of few specific attributes, the proposed project will simultaneously consider i) resource, ii) product/market and iii) value chain characteristics. The measurement approach of Pehrsson, who investigated performance differences of diversified manufacturing companies in the Swedish economy, shall be applied in the context of M&A in order to elicit the impact of relatedness on synergistic potentials and performance gains.

The research project shall furthermore examine the impact of business relatedness on different synergy types, namely i) income synergy, ii) cost synergy and iii) dyssynergy. This distinction appears important since high or low relatedness may be beneficial for different M&A objectives. As evident from the study of Swaminathan et al., high relatedness is favourable for consolidation driven M&A while low relatedness is beneficial for M&A with the objective of diversification (Swaminathan et al. 2008, p. 42). The research project shall therefore reflect the contingency framework presented by Swaminathan et al. which suggests that high relatedness favours the cost synergy, while low relatedness facilitates the realization of income synergy.

A good understanding of the synergistic potential is vital for the success of M&A. As observed by Kode et al., "many acquisitions fail to create shareholder value for the buyer [...] through either a failure to evaluate synergies at all or through payment of excessive premiums relative to the potential synergies that could be realized from the merger" (2003, p. 27). The proposed study shall provide an insight into the potential to realize certain synergies based on a given level of relatedness and as a result enable practitioners to make important predictions about the possible performance gains during the pre-merger evaluation.

3 Methodology

The purpose of the research project is to elicit the impact of business relatedness on the realization of synergy in M&A. In order to investigate the relationship between the before-mentioned concepts and to draw generalizable conclusions, it has been decided to apply a cross-sectional, hypothesis-testing survey design to empirical data. The study thus follows the methodological approach of Pehrsson's (2006a) investigation which provides vital building blocks for the research project.

3.1 Conceptual framework

The extant body of research in the field of M&A, in particular studies measuring the degree of relatedness based on product/market attributes, could not yield consistent findings on the impact of relatedness between the merging entities on the performance of M&A.

A different, more recent stream of research suggests that synergy is not only a result of similarities between the joining firms, but may also arise from the degree of complementarity between the joining firms (Larsson and Finkelstein 1999). As apparent from the study of Swaminathan (2008), the degree of similarity between the resource patterns might be more or less favourable depending on the merger motive. A high degree of similarity appears to have a positive impact on performance for M&A driven by the desire for consolidation, while differences in the resource configuration are more beneficial for diversification. This implies that a high level of relatedness should facilitate the realization of cost synergies, since cost rationalization is the primary objective to pursue consolidation-based transactions (Swaminathan et al. 2008, p. 37). Conversely, the findings of the study suggest that low relatedness might be more beneficial for the realization of income synergy, since deficiencies in certain key resources of the acquiring firm are more likely to be overcome by the acquisition of a target company with dissimilar resource patterns. The same is true for mature, slow-growing companies with excess resources which would like to explore new growth opportunities. The probability of achieving additional income should be highest if the excess resources are deployed to a firm which has deficiencies in the relevant areas (Swaminathan et al. 2008, p. 38).

The proposed study shall therefore further elicit the degree to which business relatedness will impact the realization of income and cost synergy. In contrast to Swaminathan et al. (2008), who only considered the similarity of two resources (marketing, research and development), it is planned to investigate the impact of business relatedness simultaneously for a number of different product/market, resource and value chain attributes. This approach is justified by recent contributions in the field which argue in favour of a multi-dimensional measurement of the concept of relatedness (Stimpert and Duhaime 1997; Pehrsson 2006a; Pehrsson 2006b). The research project will therefore address the criticism of the conventional conceptualization of business relatedness and make a crucial contribution to the extant body of research which has predominantly captured relatedness through a limited number of attributes (Stimpert and Duhaime 1997, p. 112).

In the conceptual model (see figure 3-1), the concept of business relatedness resembles the independent variable. In line with Pehrsson, the variable shall be measured through five dimensions, namely product technology, end customers, general management skills, brand recognition and supply channels based on the perceptions of M&A experts. The level of synergy realized in M&A forms the dependent variable of the study. In order to investigate the impact of business relatedness on different synergy types, it was decided to determine the degree of income and cost synergy separately. Since the sharing of value activities with the objective to create synergy is only useful if the benefits exceed the cost of sharing (Porter 1985, p. 324), it was planned to capture the level of dyssynergy separately in addition to income and cost synergy.

The extent of synergy realization largely depends on the post-merger integration (Larsson and Finkelstein 1999, p. 6). In the study by Homburg and Bucerius (2006), it has been found that the speed of integration has a significant effect on M&A performance depending on the degree of relatedness. Hence, it is expected that the speed of integration will moderate the relationship between business relatedness and synergy realization.

Figure 3-1: Conceptual model of the research project

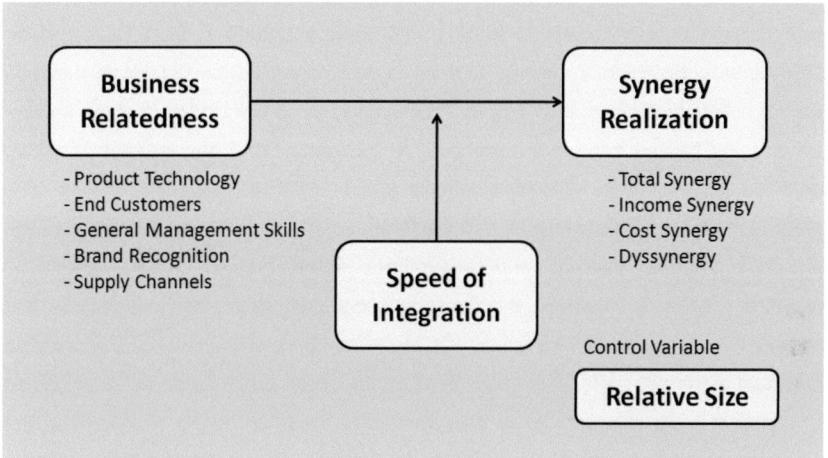

Source: Researcher

The extent of synergy realization is furthermore influenced by the size of the acquired firm. In order to generate sizeable synergies, it is required that the target company has a significant relative size compared to the acquirer (Chatterjee 1986, p. 125; Seth 1990, p. 108). It is therefore planned to control for the relative size in the conceptual model.

3.1.1 Dependent variable

Many research projects in the field have investigated the impact of relatedness on M&A performance based on stock-return measures (Chatterjee 1986; Singh and Montgomery 1987; Sirower 1997). The focus of the proposed research project is however to elicit the relationship between key attributes of the merging firms on the realization of synergy which is the dependent variable of the study. As synergy is created from linkages in the value chain and the sharing of resources, it was planned to survey executives who had an in-depth insight into the relevant M&A transactions.

As regards the quantification of synergy, the extant literature proposes two different approaches (Lechner and Meyer 2003, p. 312; Hofmann 2004, p. 263). Based on the direct approach, the total synergy amount is determined as the difference between the net present values of the merged entities and the combined value of the individual merging parties prior to the merger. On the other hand, the indirect approach identifies the individual synergistic effects and sums their respective values. The direct approach offers the benefit that the total synergy amount is determined as the difference between the pre- and post-merger states, thereby eliminating various valuation problems. However, the direct valuation approach does not provide any visibility of the individual synergistic effects. A transparent overview of the possible individual synergistic effects is considered an important prerequisite so as to devise an effective integration plan as well as to monitor the post-merger realization of the synergies. If applied correctly to the same transaction, both direct and indirect valuation approaches should yield the same result. The valuation of synergies can be integrated with common acquisition valuation methods (Lechner and Meyer 2003, p. 312). In the case of a discounted cash flow valuation, which is the most commonly applied valuation approach (Mukherjee et al. 2004, p. 16), the individual synergistic effects can be reflected as income and cost synergies using the indirect valuation approach (Hofmann 2004, p. 264). Accordingly, it is planned to measure the extent of realized income and cost synergies. Furthermore, given the significance of adverse effects related to the integration of previously independent firms, it is planned to measure the extent of dyssynergies arising. All individual synergistic effects shall be measured using a five point Likert scale with the following response categories: i) very high, ii) high, iii) medium, iv) low and v) very low.

3.1.2 Independent variable

The degree of business relatedness constitutes the independent variable of the study. The construct of business relatedness has been operationalized in Pehrsson's (2006a) study and whose measurement approach shall be adopted for this research project.

Based on a content analysis of the extant literature, Pehrsson identified 16 attributes of business relatedness. By means of factor analysis of the data collected with a final sample of 124 questionnaires, the author resolved on six underlying factors of business relatedness, namely i) product technology, ii) general management skills, iii) end customers, iv) brand recognition, v) supply channel types and vi) market knowledge (Pehrsson 2006a, p. 272). The item reliability of the measure was tested by Pehrsson using Cronbach's coefficient alpha which indicates the degree of internal consistency of various items in a scale (Tharenou et al. 2007, p. 153). With the exception of the factor vi) market knowledge, all individual factors have shown an alpha value of at least 0.60 which is considered the acceptable minimum for exploratory studies and newly developed scales (Cavana, Delahaye and Sekaran 2001, p. 324; Tharenou et al. 2007, p. 153). For the purpose of the study, it was decided to consider only the five factors with a minimum alpha value of 0.60 as illustrated in figure 3-2. The five factors are captured based on multi-item measures with a total of 14 individual attributes of relatedness (see Appendix I for the individual survey questions in the research instrument).

Figure 3-2: Factors underlying business relatedness

Factors:	Factor 1 Product Technology	Factor 2 General Management Skills	Factor 3 End Customers	Factor 4 Brand Recognition	Factor 5 Supply Channel Types
Cronbach Alpha:	0.79	0.83	0.72	0.71	0.60
Items:	• Product Technology • Product Use • Product Design • Pricing	• General Management Skills • Technical Skills • Administrative Skills	• End Customer Types • Sales Channel Types • After Sales Services	• Brand Recognition • Brand Identity	• Supply Channel Types • Suppliers

Source: Adapted from Pehrsson 2006a, p. 272

In the survey, the respondents were asked to evaluate the similarity of the merging firms with regards to the 14 items based on their own perception using a five point Likert scale in line with Pehrsson's study, with following response categories: i) very similar, ii) similar, iii) medium, iv) different and v) very different.

3.1.3 Moderating variable

M&A with the objective of synergy realization, require the integration of the independent firms to establish the value chain linkages for sharing of skills and resources. The post-merger integration process is therefore often viewed as a critical factor to achieving synergy (Larsson and Finkelstein 1999, p. 1; Gerdes 2000, p. 5).

The meta-analysis of Kode, Ford and Sutherland (2003) shows that a slow pace of post-merger integration is commonly viewed as a key reason for failed M&A projects, since synergies are only realized gradually while the purchase price is usually paid upfront in one payment together with a possible acquisition premium. As future synergistic gains must be valued in present time when compared to the acquisition premium, any delay in the realization of synergies can adversely affect the success of a transaction for the shareholders of the buying firm (Kode et al. 2003, p. 31).

A more recent research project conducted by Homburg and Bucerius (2006) how-ever questions the common belief that a quick integration is always positively corre-lated with M&A success. The researchers argue that the benefit of a swift imple-mentation of changes is contingent on the degree of relatedness between the merg-ing entities. With regards to external, market-related issues, it is argued that cus-tomer uncertainty will be higher for M&A with low relatedness which exhibit signifi-cant differences between the merging entities concerning target markets and market positioning. Based on the data collected with a final sample of 232 executives re-sponsible for post-merger integration, the researchers revealed that the beneficial effects of a rapid integration project are in fact particularly strong in the case of low external relatedness, which provides support to the notion that the uncertainty of customers with regards to merger-related policy changes can be resolved more quickly (Homburg and Bucerius 2006, p. 350).

Accordingly, it is expected that the speed of the post-merger integration will have a positive moderating effect on synergy creation in the case of low business related-ness. The speed of the integration is measured based on five point Likert scales with the following response categories: i) less than 6 months, ii) 6-12 months, iii) 13-18 months, iv) 19-24 months and v) more than 24 months (Homburg and Bucerius 2006, p. 364). An additional category was added to account for acquisitions which have not been integrated.

3.1.4 Control variables

To avoid spurious data, it is important to control for effects which might distort the relationship between the main variables in the conceptual model (Tharenou et al. 2007, p. 9).

The extant literature suggests that M&A performance is affected by the relative size of the acquiring and target firms. It is argued that the potential to generate synergies is higher for target firms which have a significant size compared to the acquiring firm (Chatterjee 1986, p. 125; Seth 1990, p. 108).

> *Any synergy that is generated by the merger is limited by the size of the target firm. For example, any operational synergy is limited by the economies of scale/scope that the (post-merger) target firm is capable of generating. The amount of synergy present should thus be correlated with the target firm's size and hence can be proxied by it. Similarly, any capital infusion provided by the acquiring firm is useful only to the point that it can be absorbed by the target (Chatterjee 1986, p. 125).*

Asquith, Bruner and Mullins (1983, cited in: Bruner 2002, p. 56) report findings which are consistent with the size effect. In their study, the researchers found that the returns to buyers are positively related to the relative size of the merging entities. Likewise, Sirower revealed a significant positive effect of the relative size of the merging entities on post-merger performance (Sirower 1997, p. 171). The relevance of the size effect is underpinned by Kitching (1967, p. 86) who found in his research project that 84% of the M&A projects which have exhibited a size mismatch (target company's sales were less than 2% of the acquirer's sales), were considered failures.

Hence, it is planned to control for the relative size of the target firm compared to the acquiring company which shall be measured in terms of the annual turnover using a five point Likert scale with the following response categories: i) more than 100%, ii) 75-100%, iii) 50-74%, iv) 25-49% and v) less than 25% (Homburg and Bucerius 2006, p. 354).

3.2   Research questions and hypotheses

Based on the inconsistencies in the literature, the research project will focus on the following research questions:

1. To what extent does business relatedness impact synergy in M&A?

2. To what extent does the speed of the post-merger integration project influence synergy realization?

3. What is the planning accuracy and effectiveness of dyssynergy?

4. What is the impact of diversification on M&A performance?

To address the research questions, it is planned to test a total number of ten hypotheses which have been formulated based on the literature.

Swaminathan et al. found that similar resource patterns are more beneficial for consolidation-based mergers which are pursued by acquirers "to strengthen their positions in existing product markets" (2008, p. 37). The rationale behind this finding is the notion that the scope for cost efficiencies is higher in related M&A through the combination of similar resources (Swaminathan et al. 2008, p. 37). This finding is corroborated by Chatterjee who argues that "there is strong and uniform academic evidence that horizontal industry consolidations, motivated by capacity reductions, are one of the few merger categories that seem to succeed" (Chatterjee 2007, p. 49). Therefore, the following hypothesis was formulated:

H1: High business relatedness will facilitate cost synergy.

In turn, Swaminathan et al. (2008) revealed that different resource patterns support value creation in diversification-based M&A. Since diversification is motivated by the objective to find alternative applications for existing resources, differences in the resource configurations between the merging entities are considered beneficial for conglomerate transactions. Alternatively, a firm which is deficient in key resources can address their needs by acquiring a target company with complementary resources. In conglomerate M&A, the merging firms typically lack familiarity with each other's industries which makes it more difficult to identify redundancies and to realize cost synergy (Swaminathan et al. 2008, p. 38). There it is assumed that the value gains observed by Swaminathan are primarily attributed to income synergy. This notion is supported by Hofmann who relates income synergies to advantages derived from differentiation of products and resources (Hofmann 2004, p. 280). Hence, the following hypothesis was formulated:

H2: Low business relatedness will facilitate income synergy.

Based on a meta-analysis of 10 merger studies, Lubatkin (1983) shows that horizontal M&A on average exhibit the highest synergistic benefits. The author argues that the performance gains to the acquiring firm are largely contingent on the degree of unifying features between the merging firms (Lubatkin 1983, p. 218). Similarly, Singh and Montgomery (1987) found in a subsequent study that related acquisitions on average outperform unrelated transactions. The researchers reason that the superior performance gains in related M&A are realized through sharing of resources which enable the merged entity to exploit economies of scale, economies of scope as well as benefits from increased market power. In turn, efficiency gains in unrelated M&A are limited to the absence of product/market and technological relationships between the merging firms (Singh and Montgomery 1987, p. 379). While conflicting evidence needs to be appreciated (Lubatkin 1987; Seth 1990), the "literature views related acquisitions more favourably than conglomerate acquisitions in terms of shareholder wealth creation for both bidders and targets (Datta et al. 1992, p. 71)." The academic debate was therefore revisited by testing the following hypothesis:

H3: High business relatedness will facilitate total synergy.

Significant support was found in Pehrsson's study for the relationship between firm performance and technological relatedness (Pehrsson 2006a, p. 277). Companies with high technological relatedness exhibit similarities concerning product features, namely product use, product design, product technology and pricing (Pehrsson 2006a, p. 272). The researcher argues that the positive performance effect of high technological relatedness is a consequence of the accumulated competence achieved through consistent investments in facilities, personnel and intellectual property in a certain product field. High technological relatedness will allow the firm to exploit operational synergies in similar fields and therefore conditions its future profitability (Pehrsson 2006a, p. 275). In other words, firms with high technological relatedness benefit from a "core competency of technology that provides potential access to many markets, makes a significant contribution to the perceived customer benefit of the end product, and is difficult to imitate" (Prahalad and Hamel 1990, cited in: Pehrsson 2006a, p. 278).

SIC codes, which are commonly used to establish the degree of relatedness, are also based on product technology assuming that two business units which share the same SIC codes must have similar product attributes (Pehrsson 2006b, p. 354).

However, the assumption that two businesses within the same two-digit SIC codes are in any case related is questioned by researchers. Robins and Wiersema argue that the SIC system lacks content validity since the "links between the measures and the concept of portfolio 'relatedness' are uncertain" (Robins and Wiersema 2003, p. 58). Hence, categorical measures like the SIC system can be considered a measure of diversification rather than relatedness (Hoskisson, Hitt, Johnson and Moesel 1993, p. 218).

Furthermore, it can be noted that SIC codes may determine relatedness as viewed by external observers while neglecting strategic aspects. However, strategic decisions strongly rely on the perception of relatedness as viewed by the management which might differ from external observations (Pehrsson 2006b, p. 355). Since M&A resemble a strategic option for the firm, the study will investigate whether the relationship between firm performance and technological relatedness, based on managerial perceptions as shown by Pehrsson for diversified manufacturing companies, is also true in the context of synergistic M&A, by testing the following hypothesis:

H4: High business relatedness concerning product technology will increase total synergy.

The prevailing theme of past research has been the notion that acquisitions between firms which exhibit similarities in terms of their product/market presence have the greatest probability to achieve synergy and enhance shareholder value (Harrison et al. 1991, p. 186). However, empirical studies using product/market measures of relatedness did not succeed in revealing a consistent relationship between relatedness and firm performance (Chatterjee 1986; Lubatkin 1987; Singh and Montgomery 1987). Harrison et al. (1991) concluded that the conflicting findings are related to the fact that similarities are likely known by rival firms prompting them to participate in the bidding process. This, in turn, increases the purchase price and hence causes the majority of the value gains to be transferred to the shareholders of the target firm. Instead, the researchers elaborate that complementarities in the resource allocation patterns are more relevant to create private, unique and valuable synergies which are much less prone to result in an auction and are less imitable by competing firms

(Harrison et al. 1991, p. 187). This notion is underscored by Hitt et al. (1998) who found in their research project that successful acquisitions exposed complementary resources.

> *The key to success appears to be the ability to identify complementarities and take specific actions to achieve positive synergy (noticeably absent in the unsuccessful acquisitions). Thus, resource complementarities are of greater importance than the product/market relatedness of a specific acquisition (Hitt et al. 1998, p. 107).*

The impact of resource relatedness on the performance of foreign subsidiaries was investigated by Pehrsson (2009) in a sample of 191 companies wholly owned by Swedish manufacturing firms. The study focused on skills relatedness as a crucial intangible resource in the exploitation of core competence. The author argues that the performance gains from related skills are realized through learning which results in "increased knowledge in each business line, and in gains through cost reduction, increased differentiation and sales" (Farjoun 1998, cited in: Pehrsson 2009, p. 11). The variable *skills relatedness* was established through four items, namely i) management skills, ii) technical skills, iii) marketing skills and iv) administrative skills. The data revealed a significant positive impact of skills relatedness on subsidiary performance while product/market relatedness did not show a significant relationship. The author argues that intangible resources are embodied in individuals who transform core competencies from the parent company to the subsidiary. The higher the relatedness in terms of skills, the more susceptible the subsidiary becomes to exploit the core competency of the parent firm (Pehrsson 2009, p. 23). In the context of M&A, it is likewise expected that resource relatedness will facilitate synergy through learning and the exploitation of core competencies between the merging parties. Therefore, the following hypothesis was tested:

H5: High relatedness concerning resource attributes will increase total synergy.

A study conducted by KPMG on a sample of 107 companies illustrates that income synergy is less likely to occur than cost synergy (KPMG 1999, p. 12). This finding is corroborated by an analysis conducted on data from a client survey of McKinsey (Early 2004) which has revealed that 70% of M&A fail to achieve the expected income synergies as opposed to only 20% for cost synergies. It is argued that this finding is largely related to difficulties in estimating income synergies which, unlike cost synergy, requires the management to anticipate the behaviour of customers and competitors (Early 2004, p. 9). The notion that the realization of cost synergy has a higher success rate as opposed to income synergy is supported by a study of 208 bank mergers during the period 1985-1992 which found higher market discounts for M&A realized in pursuit of revenue synergies compared to cost synergies (Houston and Ryngaert 1996, p. 76). Likewise, a meta-analysis of the consulting literature showed that revenue growth declined post-merger in the majority of cases (Pautler 2003, p. 4). In summary, the extant literature provides strong support for the notion that "synergies in cost reductions are easier than revenue increase" (Chatterjee 2007, p. 49). Therefore, the following hypothesis was tested:

H6: Overall, cost synergy is more likely to occur than income synergy in M&A.

Synergy can only be created in the presence of organizational integration (Larsson and Finkelstein 1999, p. 6). In this context, a recent study found that the speed of integration is most beneficial for transactions with low relatedness while being detrimental in the presence of high relatedness (Homburg and Bucerius 2006). The researchers argue that this finding is mainly caused by customer uncertainty which increases in M&A with low external relatedness due to a potential repositioning of the product offering (Homburg and Bucerius 2006, p. 350). The loss of customers during the post-merger integration can result in significant income dyssynergies (Hofmann 2004, p. 293). Hence, the following hypothesis was formulated:

H7: Speed of integration will facilitate synergy for M&A with low business relatedness.

During the post-merger integration, it is required that the management takes specific actions to realize the planned synergistic effects. These measures might result in negative performance effects which are referred to as negative synergy or dyssynergy. In other words, each positive synergistic effect might require additional expenditures before the benefits can be captured. The relevance of a careful analysis of dyssynergies is underpinned by Porter who highlights that the sharing of value chain activities is only reasonable if the "advantage of sharing outweighs the cost" (Porter 1985, p. 326).

Dyssynergy might occur in the form of additional cost or reduced income as already discussed in the literature review section. Moreover, the efforts to realize synergy might result in increased risk to the combined entity. This may be the case if the profit development of the merged operations is highly correlated (systematic risk), or if the consolidation of resources increases the susceptibility to natural disaster and total destruction of certain production factors (unsystematic risk) (Rodermann 1999, p. 210). The detrimental effects in the context of synergistic M&A have been discussed in greater detail by Shaver (2006) and Lechner (2007a).

As a result, it can be noted that the establishment of linkages between two entities has the potential to cause significant dyssynergies. "The potential for value creation must therefore always be balanced against the risk of value destruction" (Campbell, Goold and Alexander 1995, p. 81). Furthermore, it can be observed that corporate executives tend to have an upside bias towards positive synergy while neglecting possible impediments. "The downsides of synergy are [however] every bit as real as the upsides; they are just not seen as clearly" (Goold and Campbell 1998, p. 136). Many acquirers do not conduct a proper risk analysis and instead pursue optimistic planning assumptions in order "to make the numbers justify the deal" (Eccles et al. 1999, p. 144). As a result, acquirers often grossly underestimate the negative implications associated with mergers (Early 2004, p. 9). Based on the above mentioned argument, the following two hypotheses were tested in the research project:

H8: Dyssynergies are on average underestimated in the pre-merger evaluation.

H9: M&A with high dyssynergies are more likely to diminish shareholder value.

One area of research which has received considerable attention is the relationship between corporate diversification and financial performance (Prahalad and Bettis 1986, p. 485). Various empirical studies support the notion that M&A with the objective to pursue diversification, on average destroy value (Morck, Shleifer and Vishny 1990; Walker 2000; Lamont and Polk 2001). A key explanation for this phenomenon is that conglomerates tend to misallocate funds to subsidize unprofitable business units (Mukherjee et al. 2004, p. 10). It is also argued by scholars active in the field that the realization of operating synergy is very limited in diversification based M&A (Singh and Montgomery 1987, p. 380). Horizontal organizations, on the other hand, have the opportunity to successfully implement linkages between the value chains and realize benefits from the sharing of resources (Ensign 1998, p. 660). Moreover, diversifications are on average associated with a higher risk since the management of the acquiring firm has limited knowledge about the industry and market of the target firm (Datta et al. 1992, p. 79). "On the whole, [the] literature views related acquisitions more favourably than conglomerate acquisitions in terms of shareholder wealth creation for both bidders and targets" (Datta et al. 1992, p. 71). A more recent stream of empirical studies however contests the general notion that diversification on average destroys value (Campa and Kedia 2002; Villalonga 2004). The researchers argue that the findings of past research projects are caused by selectivity bias. If adjusted for these effects, diversification-based M&A are not less favourable than related M&A (Mukherjee et al. 2004, p. 10). The research project revisited this issue and investigated the overall profitability of related and unrelated M&A by testing the following hypothesis:

H10: Horizontal M&A create more shareholder value for the shareholders of the acquiring firm than diversification-based M&A.

3.3 Sampling and research instrument

Studies investigating the profitability of M&A projects can be classified into four different research approaches, namely i) event studies, ii) accounting studies, iii) surveys of managers and iv) case studies (Bruner 2002, p. 49).

Event studies, which are also referred to as market-based studies, examine the development of the share price of the merging entities surrounding the announcement of a transaction. The key measure of event studies is typically the abnormal return to the shareholders, which is the change in share price and any dividends paid in relation to a benchmark, such as a market index. This research approach is considered forward-looking since the share price in theory reflects the present value of the expected future cash flows. Event studies offer a direct measure of the value created for shareholders based on data which is readily available. On the other hand, market-based studies require significant assumptions concerning the functioning of the stock market and are vulnerable to confounding events which might distort the share price development (Bruner 2002, p. 51).

Accounting studies are based on the review of financial statements and are therefore considered backward-looking. Different measures can be applied to determine the financial performance following an acquisition, such as net income, return on equity or return on assets. Accounting studies offer the benefit that financial statements are easily available for large corporations, and are usually audited and thus deemed a reliable source of information. In turn, financial statements may suffer from changes in accounting policies and other events which might affect the comparability of data over time (Bruner 2002, p. 51; Hofmann 2004, p. 227).

Surveys of managers interview executives who are familiar with the acquisition process. This research approach benefits from the intimate familiarity of the respondents with a specific M&A project and yields insights into the value creation process which cannot be generated through event and accounting studies. Surveys with managers however suffer from low response rates (Bruner 2004, p. 51). Moreover, it can be noticed that past studies using this research approach have predominantly reported successful M&A projects which suggests a positive bias of managers who have a direct stake in the relevant transaction (Hofmann 2004, p. 233).

Case studies are typically confined to a small sample of transactions which are analyzed in greater depth mainly using field interviews. While this research approach offers the possibility to yield new insights, it is not suitable to hypothesis-testing research designs and generalization due to the small number of observations (Bruner 2004, p.51).

The purpose of the proposed study demands an in-depth view into an M&A project throughout the entire transaction. In particular, it is required that the respondents can express a qualified opinion on the resource configuration of the merging entities as well as the extent of the planned and realized synergies which necessitates executives familiar with the M&A process. One objective of the study is to yield generaliz-able conclusions and to test hypotheses generated from the extant literature. Based on the strengths and weaknesses of the different research approaches outlined above, it was decided to conduct a survey with managers. Unlike Pehrsson's study, which was based on a survey with managers of the relevant firms, it was planned to survey M&A consultants. This approach was expected to reduce the positive bias observed in surveys with corporate managers. Furthermore, it was expected that the evaluation of intermediaries would be less industry specific and based on a broader experience with M&A projects relevant for making judgements (Walter and Barney 1990, p. 79).

The survey was conducted with the International Network of Mergers & Acquisitions Partner (IMAP) which is a partnership of 60 independent advisory firms specialized in medium-sized transactions and located in 35 countries in Asia/Pacific, Europe and North and South America with its head office in Sarasota, Florida, USA. In 2007, IMAP firms completed a total number of 254 transactions with an average transac-tion volume of 39.2 m USD (IMAP 2008). Given the global scope of the survey, it was decided to use a web-based questionnaire for the survey. A web-based survey offered the advantage of being more cost efficient than a mail survey which requires postage. Furthermore, the respondents were more easily invited by email and the laborious and error-prone data entry associated with mail questionnaires was not required for the online survey. The questionnaire was administered based on a cen-sus sample to all 319 M&A partners worldwide. The invitation to participate in the study was sent out by the Chairman of IMAP by email including a web-link to access the online survey.

The survey questions that tapped into the construct of relatedness had been devel-oped based on the questionnaire used by Pehrsson (2006a). The similarity of the merging entities concerning 14 key attributes was measured using a five point Likert scale (ranging from 1 = very similar; to 5 = very different). Given that Pehrsson's research design using managerial perceptions was of an exploratory nature, it was decided to add an established measure of relatedness into the research project to reveal possible inconsistencies in the measurement approach. The FTC classification appeared useful for this purpose since it was simple, readily available and in line with the common terminology used in the field of M&A. Accordingly, mergers were classified into four categories, namely i) horizontal and horizontal with market extension, ii) horizontal with product extension, iii) vertical and iv) conglomerate. The category of market concentric mergers was grouped together with horizontal M&A given the ease with which a firm can extend their geographical markets in today's environment (Howell 1970, p. 67; Lubatkin 1987, p. 41). The FTC classification was used to describe the sample as well as to reveal any inconsistencies in the measurement of relatedness using managerial perceptions.

In line with the concept of relatedness, the degree of synergy achieved in the respective M&A projects was measured using a five point Likert scale (ranging from 1 = very high; to 5 = very low). In addition to the extent of total synergy achieved, the degree of income and cost synergy as well as dyssynergy was measured through separate survey questions in order to test for the impact of relatedness on these particular synergy types. As the success of M&A projects in terms of value enhancement is largely contingent on the fact that the expected value gains factored in the purchase price evaluation are captured following the merger, it was decided to establish the variance of the extent of the realized synergies compared to the expected synergies prior to the merger (KPMG 2006, p. 2). Using a five point Likert scale, the degree to which the actual income and cost synergies met the expectations was measured (ranging from 1 = failed significantly; to 5 = exceeded significantly). Furthermore, the respondents were questioned about whether dyssynergies had been considered in the pre-merger evaluation and how the actual dyssynergies compared to the planned amounts (ranging from 1 = significantly lower; to 5 = significantly higher). In line with the survey conducted by KPMG (2006), the overall success of the M&A projects was established through three categories, namely i) created shareholder value, ii) preserved shareholder value and iii) diminished shareholder value.

3.4   Data analysis and statistical tests

Before elaborating on the individual methods applied in this study, it is necessary to discuss the measurement scales which determine the appropriate statistical tests.

Nominal, ordinal, interval and ratio scales of measurement can be differentiated (Tharenou et al. 2007, p. 193). Nominal data classifies data into two or more mutually exclusive groups, while ordinal scales additionally provide the order of the groups. Interval and ratio scales are quantitative and reflect a linear relationship with the underlying variable measured, yet an absolute zero is not available for interval scales of measurement (Tharenou et al. 2007, p. 193). Another common way to classify data is to distinguish between categorical and continuous variables. Categorical variables sort two or more distinct groups or categories in an ordered or unordered manner, while continuous variables take on quantitative values which reflect the amount of the variable. Categorical variables are measured on nominal or ordinal scales, whereas continuous variables have interval or ratio scales of measurement (Tharenou et al. 2007, p. 194). In line with Pehrsson (2006a), the degree of relatedness was captured using five point Likert scales. Similarly, all other variables required for the testing of hypotheses were measured using Likert scales or categorical items which provided the magnitude between the responses. The data generated for the statistical tests was therefore measured on ordinal scales which can be arranged in order of ranks, while the difference between the ranks cannot be quantified (Cavana et al. 2001, p. 196).

At the outset of the statistical analysis, the data will be described using frequency distributions. Thereafter, the correlation of the individual variables shall be illustrated using a correlation matrix in order to obtain an indication of the initial relationship between the dependent and independent variables. The correlation of ordinal variables can be established with specific tests, such as the Spearman's rank correlation coefficient (Tharenou et al. 2007, p. 208). However, in order to allow for a direct comparison of the survey results to the research findings of Pehrsson (2006a), it has been decided to apply Pearson's correlation coefficient which is most commonly known in organizational research (Tharenou et al. 2007, p. 207). Pearson's correlation coefficient describes the strength and direction of the linear relationship between two variables. The coefficient ranges from '-1' to '+1', whereby '0' denotes no association and '-1' and '+1' represent a perfect correlation between the variables. The application of Pearson's correlation coefficient demands dichotomous or continuous variables. However, in the case of five or more response categories, Likert scales are commonly viewed and evaluated as a continuous scale (Tharenou et al. 2007, p. 193).

The concept of business relatedness has been captured using multi-measure items. In order to prepare the data for the subsequent statistical analysis, it is required to aggregate the individual items to the five dimensions of relatedness by computing the mean value of the respective items. Moreover, since the general impact of relatedness on synergy realization shall be examined, it is necessary to aggregate the five dimensions further to an overall score of relatedness by calculating the mean value of the individual dimensions (Tharenou et al. 2007, p. 161).

The effectiveness of relatedness on M&A performance shall be examined using a two step approach. Firstly, the impact of the overall relatedness on synergy realization will be investigated based on an analysis of variance using the aggregated score of relatedness. Secondly, the influence of the individual dimensions of relatedness on synergy realization will be tested with the help of multiple regression analysis.

An analysis of variance (Iversen and Norpoth 1987) shall be applied to test whether the extent of synergy realization is different for transactions with varying degree of the overall relatedness. The statistical test helps to examine whether a significant mean difference exists among two or more groups on a dependent variable as indicated by the F statistic. The F statistic reflects the ratio of the variance between groups divided by the within-group variance. The greater the likelihood of between group variances as opposed to within-group variance, the higher the likelihood that the means of the two groups are significantly different (Cavana et al. 2001, p. 430).

Subsequently, the impact of the individual dimensions of relatedness on synergy realization will be examined using multiple regression analysis (Cohen, Cohen, West and Aiken 2003). The regression analysis applied in this study is the ordinary least squares regression which is the most commonly used regression analysis. It determines the extent of the relationship of two or more independent variables with a dependent variable using a least squares estimation procedure. The strength and direction of the influence of the independent variables is indicated by the coefficient. The statistical significance shall be determined using a two-tailed t-test (Tharenou et al. 2007, p. 223). The proportion of variance in the dependent variable explained by the set of independent variable is determined by the multiple R^2. This statistic provides an indication of the predictive power of the statistical model. The R^2 can assume a value between '0' and '1', whereas a value close to '1' indicates that the statistical model fits the data well. In the subject study, the adjusted R^2 shall be calculated which takes into account the degrees of freedom in the individual tests (Cavana et al. 2001, p. 436). In order to minimize sample loss in the multiple regression analysis, it is planned to delete missing data pairwise (Tharenou et al. 2007, p. 225). Furthermore, it shall be examined whether the data suffers from multicollinearity which occurs when two or more independent variables are highly correlated. A common approach to check for multicollinearity is the computation of Variance Inflation Factors (VIF) whereby VIF > 10 indicates that the relevant variable might be redundant (Kline 2005, p. 57).

Lastly, Fisher's (1935) exact test shall be applied to examine the statistical significance of contingency tables. The statistical test determines the association between two categorical variables. Fisher's exact is deemed to be more appropriate than the chi-square test since it provides an exact significance value rather than an approximation. Furthermore, Fisher's exact test is more robust for small sample sizes (Everitt 1992, p. 14).

A significance level of 5 percent ($p<0.05$), which is most commonly used in business and management research, shall be applied to all statistical tests (Cavana et al. 2001, p. 415).

3.5   Reliability and validity

Irrespective of the type of research design, it is paramount that the measures applied in the study are reliable and valid. Reliability gauges whether a certain measure is free from random measurement error, while validity ascertains whether the researcher is in fact tapping into the construct of interest (Tharenou et al. 2007, p. 24).

Internal validity refers to the degree of confidence that the researcher can place in the cause-effect relationship between two variables. The impact of the concept of relatedness on firm performance, which is the focal point of this study, has been extensively researched over the past decades (Chatterjee 1986; Lubatkin 1987; Singh and Montgomery 1987). While the findings are largely contradictory, the overall body of research however suggests that the degree of relatedness in fact plays a vital role on the performance of the diversified firm (Bruner 2004, p. 69).

The term internal validity has slightly different meanings in quantitative and qualitative research (Punch 1998, p. 29). As regards quantitative studies, the issue of validity is also referred to as *measurement validity* which is typically established through three main approaches, namely i) content validity, ii) criterion validity and iii) construct validity (Punch 1998, p. 97). The internal validity of the study has been evaluated using content validity which addresses the question whether a measure adequately covers the relevant domain of interest. It can be estimated through a thorough review of the relevant literature or consultation with subject matter experts (Tharenou et al. 2007, p. 157).

The phenomenon of synergy is conceptualized in numerous ways in the extant literature (Ropella 1989, p. 21). However, any operational synergies eventually reflect in terms of income and cost effects (Trautwein 1990, p. 284). In particular in the context of M&A, it is a common approach to capture synergy in terms of income and cost (Lechner and Meyer 2003; Hofmann 2004; Sirower and Sahni 2006). The understanding of synergy in the field of M&A is highlighted by Chatterjee who argues that "typically the justification for such mergers or acquisitions is that [...] their union can lead to an increase in revenue (revenue synergy), efficiency (cost synergy), or both" (2007, p. 46). Accordingly, the concept of synergy has been measured in terms of income and cost synergy. In addition, the degree of dyssynergy has been measured, in order to account for any detrimental effects incurred during the post-merger integration (Hofmann 2004; Hofmann 2005; Lechner 2007b).

The concept of relatedness is typically captured through either SIC-based product-count measures or categorical measures as developed by Rumelt (Montgomery 1982, p. 299). These measurement approaches have however been criticized for being unable to capture the complex phenomenon of relatedness between firms (Keats 1990, p. 69). Recent contributions therefore advocate a multi-dimensional conceptualization of relatedness measuring various relevant attributes (Stimpert and Duhaime 1997; Pehrsson 2006a; Pehrsson 2006b). It has therefore been decided to adopt the measurement approach of Pehrsson (2006a) who has captured relatedness as a multi-dimensional concept based on product/market, resource and value chain attributes. The research instrument has been reviewed by subject matter experts and fellow researchers prior to launching the survey to ensure that the questionnaire was sufficiently clear.

The term external validity deals with the question whether the findings of the research project are generalizable. The problem of generalizability is particularly relevant to case study designs which often suffer from a small number of cases as well as idiosyncratic settings and therefore render generalizable conclusions inappropriate (Tharenou et al. 2007, p. 82). The generalizability can be increased through an elaborate sampling design (Cavana et al. 2001, p. 31). In the proposed research project, a correlational field study design has been chosen with a large sample of experts familiar with the subject matter to ensure a sufficiently high level of generalizability. Nevertheless, it has to be pointed out that there are limitations to the applicability of the results of the study. As highlighted by Lubatkin, "no study [...] is both generalizable and totally accurate; trade-offs must be recognized between the representativeness of the results and the confidence in them" (Lubatkin 1987, p. 50). This statement is particularly true for studies investigating the causes of M&A performance. There are numerous variables which influence the post-merger performance of the firm (cf. meta-analyses of Datta et al. 1992; Bruner 2002). While the study controls for the relative size of the merging firms, there are likely to be other influencing factors which have not been explicitly considered in the research design. The generalizability of the findings of this study is therefore limited by these constraints.

While validity is dealing with the relationship between concept and indicator, the issue of reliability is focusing on whether a measure is providing consistent results in repeated trials (Carmines and Zeller 1979, p. 11). The concept of synergy has been measured using a single-item scale based on a five point Likert scale. In the research instrument administered in this study, the respondents have been asked to rate the degree of realized synergy in terms of incremental income and reduced cost attributed to the M&A transaction. While the application of multi-item measures is usually preferred in academic research, sufficiently objective data, such as financial performance, is often measured by single measures (Tharenou et al. 2007, p. 163). The measure of synergy is deemed to have a sufficiently high level of reliability since income and cost constitute objective data reported in financial statements. A similar approach has been applied by Pehrsson (2009) who captured foreign subsidiary performance on a single-item measure using a three point Likert scale.

The measurement approach to the multi-dimensional concept of business relatedness is based on a study by Pehrsson (2006a). A common test to establish reliability for a multi-item measure is the internal consistency reliability. The alpha coefficient measures how individual items are related with other items in the scale (Tharenou et al. 2007, p. 152). Despite certain limitations, Cronbach's (1951) coefficient alpha remains the most widely applied measure of scale reliability (Peterson 1994, p. 381). The underlying factors of the multi-dimensional concept have been distilled into five distinctive variables using factor analysis. Four variables yield an Alpha value of more than 0.70 which is an acceptable level of reliability in business research (Cavana et al. 2001, p. 324). The variable supply chain has an alpha value of only 0.60 which is deemed sufficient for exploratory studies and newly developed scales (DeVillis 1991, cited in: Pehrsson 2006a, p. 273; Tharenou et al. 2007, p. 153). The variable market knowledge has been neglected due to insufficient internal consistency (alpha = 0.46) (Pehrsson 2006a, p. 272).

The proposed research design, which is based on interviews with insiders, is commonly criticized for their weak validity and reliability, specifically with regards to bias as a result of subjective perceptions and motivations. In turn, however, practitioners offer a valuable insight due to their intimate familiarity with the transactions (Bamberger 1994, p. 120). The research design is therefore appropriate to address the research questions put forward in this study.

3.6   Ethical considerations

Ethics in business research refers to a code of conduct, especially the application of certain norms and conventions while conducting research. Central to the discussion of ethics in business research is the relationship between the researcher and the subjects. During this relationship, which is contrived for the benefit of the researcher, the subjects will disclose information to the researcher. This situation places the researcher into a position of power and poses a risk to the subject that the information provided is disclosed to third parties and used against the subjects (Cavana et al. 2001, p. 21).

In order to safeguard the position of the subjects, it is required that the researcher obtains voluntary and informed consent from the subjects prior to launching the project. Informed consent means that subjects are aware of the goals and objectives as well as the methods applied in the study. The researcher has to provide an explanatory statement written in plain English to obtain informed consent. Inter alia, the explanatory note has to outline the purpose of the study, the expected benefits, the methods applied in the research project, the demands for potential candidates including the expectation duration, risks to the potential candidate as well as the contact name of the researcher and the ethics committee of the university (Tharenou et al. 2007, p. 320). In the research project, an electronic version of the explanatory statement is provided on the first page of the online survey. Consent is obtained from the respondents by clicking on a button which leads to the online questionnaire (Tharenou et al. 2007, p. 321). The consent of IMAP as the supporting organization has been obtained in writing prior to launching the project.

Another fundamental ethical requirement is to treat any information obtained from the subjects as strictly confidential and to preserve the privacy of the respondents (Cavana et al. 2001, p. 165). These requirements have been met by conducting an anonymous survey without any unique identifiers. The data analysis has been conducted only on an aggregated level which does not reveal individual responses (Tharenou et al. 2007, p. 320).

Prior to conducting a research project, it is required that the researcher obtains formal permission from the ethical body of the relevant institution (Tharenou et al. 2007, p. 317). The Human Research Ethics Committee of the University of South Australia, International Graduate School of Business, approved the subject research project on 14th May 2009 as being in accordance with the guidelines set by the ethics committee.

4 Data analysis and discussion

The results of the research project shall be presented in the following sequence:

First, a description of the sample is provided. Second, preliminary findings of the study will be presented based on bivariate statistics. Third, the hypotheses formulated earlier will be tested based on multivariate statistics. Last, the research findings shall be discussed based on the extant literature and limitations of the research findings are highlighted.

4.1 Univariate statistics and sample description

The data collection was conducted from 16th June 2009 until 11th November 2009. The invitation to participate in the survey was issued to 319 M&A consultants in 36 countries world-wide. During this period three reminders were sent out by the IMAP Chairman. Eventually, a final sample of 110 complete questionnaires was collected (response ratio 34.5%).

The IMAP consultants were requested to evaluate M&A projects using their recollection of the relevant transactions. Most survey questionnaires were completed by the Managing Partners (46%), while only 20 percent of the responses were provided by Managers and Associates (see table 4-1). This suggests that IMAP consultants have generally given the survey a high attention.

Table 4-1: Position of Respondents

	n	%
Managing Partner	50	45.5
Partner	34	30.9
Manager	12	10.9
Associate	10	9.1
Missing	4	3.6
N	110	100.0

Source: Researcher

The median turnover of the acquiring firms evaluated in the study amounted to 75 m EUR. Almost 90 percent of the firms reported annual sales of less than 1,000 m EUR prior to the acquisition. However, some acquiring firms realized a significantly higher annual turnover leading to mean of 636 m EUR which considerably exceeds the median value. The maximum turnover reported was 20,000 m EUR per annum. The dispersion of the number of employees is similar to the turnover. More than 50 percent of the firms reported less than 1,000 employees, while only three firms exceeded 10,000 employees. Accordingly, the sample mean of 2,569 well exceeds the median value of 410 employees. The number of employees reported ranges from 4 to 94,000 (see table 4-2).

Table 4-2: Turnover and number of employees of acquiring firms

	Mean	S.D.	Median	Min-Max
Turnover (m EUR)	636	2,219	75	1-20,000
Employees	2,569	10,298	410	4-94,000

Turnover (m EUR)	<50	50-99	100-249	250-499	500-999	>= 1,000	Missing	N
n	36	19	16	10	9	12	8	110
%	32.7	17.3	14.5	9.1	8.2	10.9	7.3	100.0

Employees	<250	250-499	500-999	1,000-4,999	5,000-9,999	>= 10,000	Missing	N
n	35	15	12	26	7	3	12	110
%	31.8	13.6	10.9	23.6	6.4	2.7	10.9	100.0

Source: Researcher

Overall, it can be noted that the sample primarily consists of medium-sized firms which are the target clientele of IMAP. The fact that there are few outliers with significantly higher turnover and number of employees is not considered to be detrimental for the purpose of the study since the relationship between relatedness and synergy realization is believed to apply to all firms regardless of their size.

In comparison, Sirower's study was conducted on a sample with an average size of the acquiring firm of 2,310 m USD which significantly exceeds the mean value of the data collected in this research project (Sirower 1997, p. 167), while the mean turnover reported in Pehrsson's study amounts to only 99 m (Pehrsson 2006a, p. 270). The differences concerning the average firm size are related to the sampling procedure. Sirower analyzed large US stock-listed companies, while Pehrsson focused on manufacturing firms in the Swedish economy.

The acquiring firms evaluated in the survey were mainly based in Europe and North America. The majority of acquiring firms originated from USA (n=25) and Germany (n=16) (see table 4-3). The regional spread of responses is a reflection of IMAP's global presence. Non-response bias with a potentially adverse impact on the research findings cannot be observed.

Table 4-3: Origin of acquiring firms

	n	%
Africa	1	0.9
Asia	4	3.6
Europe	71	64.5
Middle-East	5	4.5
North America	26	23.6
South America	2	1.8
Missing	1	0.9
N	110	100.0

Source: Researcher

The merger type was measured using the FTC classification. In line with Lubatkin (1983; 1987), the categories i) horizontal M&A and ii) horizontal M&A with market extension have been grouped together "given the ever-increasing ease of expanding one's market limits beyond existing boundaries" (Howell 1970, p. 67). This approach appears reasonable since 62 firms engaged in cross-border M&A compared to only 48 domestic transactions.

Almost 74 percent of the M&A projects evaluated in the survey were conducted within the same industry (horizontal with market / product extension), while only about 15 percent of the firms realized conglomerate transactions (see table 4-4). This suggests that the firms evaluated in the survey should typically exhibit a high degree of relatedness.

Table 4-4: FTC merger classification

	n	%
Horizontal / Horizontal with market extension	43	39.1
Horizontal with product extension	38	34.5
Vertical	13	11.8
Conglomerate / Diversification	16	14.5
N	110	100.0

Source: Researcher

The industry affiliation of the acquiring firms was established based on the Statistical Classification of Economic Activities in the European Community, Rev. 2 (NACE Rev. 2). Most acquiring firms were active in the field of manufacturing (n=46; 42 percent) (see table 4-5).

Table 4-5: Industry Classification of Acquiring Firms

	n	%
Agriculture, forestry and fishing	3	2.7
Mining and quarrying	1	0.9
Manufacturing	46	41.8
Electricity, gas, steam and air conditioning	3	2.7
Water Supply; sewerage, waste and remediation activities	1	0.9
Construction	5	4.5
Wholesale and retail trade; repair of motor vehicles and motorcycles	11	10.0
Transportation and storage	2	1.8
Information and communication	12	10.9
Financial and insurance activities	3	2.7
Real estate activities	2	1.8
Professional, scientific and technical activities	7	6.4
Administrative and support services activities	7	6.4
Education	1	0.9
Human health and social work	5	4.5
Missing	1	0.9
N	110	100.0

Source: Researcher

4.2   Bivariate statistics and preliminary findings

The relationship between the individual variables considered in the study has been calculated using Pearson's correlation coefficient. Unless otherwise stated, the correlations between the variables will be discussed at a significance level of $p < 0.01$ (see table 4-6).

As regards the dependent variables, a positive and significant relationship has been found between total synergy on the one hand and income and cost synergy on the other hand, while total synergy is negatively correlated with dyssynergy. The adverse impact of dyssynergy on the realization of total synergy is only attributable to income synergy. No significant relationship has been found between cost synergy and dyssynergy. This suggests that dyssynergy has only a detrimental effect on the realization of income synergy while cost synergy remains unaffected.

A significant positive relationship has been revealed between product technology-related variables (product use, product design, product technology and pricing) and total synergy as well as cost synergy. This finding implies that a high degree of relatedness concerning product technology will facilitate cost synergy. However, low relatedness concerning product technology will not result in income synergy.

In line with Pehrsson, a positive relationship has been detected between product technology-related and end customer-related variables (end customer types, sales channel types and after-sales services). Despite this correlation, only end customer types and after-sales services have a positive relationship with total synergy. Moreover, it appears that the impact of end customer types on total synergy is related to income synergy (significant at $p < 0.05$), while correlation between after-sales services and total synergy is caused by the realization of cost synergy (significant at $p < 0.05$).

Moreover, a significant relationship has been revealed between cost synergy and supply channel types. The higher the relatedness between the supply channels of the merging firms, the higher the realization of cost synergy. Contrary to expectation, it was found that the relative size between acquiring and target firms has a negative relationship with total synergy (significant at $p < 0.05$). This finding suggests that the realization of synergy is generally easier to accomplish for targets with a relatively smaller size compared to the acquiring firms. No significant impact has been found for the speed of the post-merger integration project.

Table 4-6: Pearson correlation coefficient

Variables	Mean	S.D.	1	2	3	4	5	6	7	8	9	10
1 Total Synergy	2.49	0.93										
2 Income Synergy	2.68	0.94	0.47***									
3 Cost Synergy	2.87	1.12	0.51***	0.04								
4 Dyssynergy	4.02	0.82	-0.35***	-0.36***	-0.11							
5 Product Use	2.29	1.29	0.40***	0.01	0.34***	0.01						
6 Product Design	2.93	1.19	0.38***	0.02	0.34***	-0.01	0.74***					
7 Product Technology	2.86	1.26	0.35***	-0.03	0.36***	-0.04	0.66***	0.76***				
8 Pricing	2.94	1.25	0.28***	0.05	0.26***	-0.03	0.57***	0.59***	0.56***			
9 General Management Skills	2.98	1.15	0.04	0.06	0.21**	-0.10	0.10	0.14	0.24**	-0.05		
10 Technical Skills	2.80	1.07	0.15	-0.01	0.23**	-0.15	0.10	0.14	0.41***	0.12	0.48***	
11 Administrative Skills	3.06	1.01	-0.06	0.09	0.05	0.00	-0.06	-0.06	0.10	-0.05	0.58***	0.39***
12 End Customer Types	2.31	1.32	0.29***	0.19**	0.11	-0.04	0.45***	0.38***	0.30***	0.48***	-0.11	0.02
13 Sales Channel Types	2.71	1.32	0.17*	0.07	0.21**	-0.03	0.29***	0.30***	0.33***	0.41***	0.26***	0.41***
14 After-sales Services	2.89	1.14	0.30***	0.11	0.25**	-0.01	0.39***	0.39***	0.43***	0.44***	0.18*	0.42***
15 Brand Recognition	3.14	1.00	0.21**	0.17*	0.15	-0.02	0.15	0.17*	0.28***	0.17*	0.17*	0.25**
16 Brand Identity	3.06	1.14	0.25**	0.10	0.17*	-0.04	0.19**	0.18*	0.30***	0.22**	0.18*	0.30***
17 Supply Channel Types	2.84	1.21	0.23**	-0.14	0.26***	0.16*	0.44***	0.48***	0.47***	0.49***	0.00	0.33***
18 Suppliers	3.00	1.29	0.23**	-0.09	0.18*	0.17*	0.40***	0.51***	0.42***	0.45***	-0.04	0.14
19 Relative Size	4.23	1.27	-0.22**	-0.01	-0.02	0.02	-0.14	-0.20**	-0.17*	-0.21**	0.17*	-0.05
20 Speed of Integration	2.35	1.08	0.05	0.18*	0.17	-0.17	-0.20*	-0.14	-0.07	-0.04	-0.06	0.01

*** p<0.01, ** p< 0.05, * p<0.1

Source: Researcher

Table 4-6: Pearson correlation coefficient (continued)

Variables	11	12	13	14	15	16	17	18	19
1 Total Synergy									
2 Income Synergy									
3 Cost Synergy									
4 Dyssynergy									
5 Product Use									
6 Product Design									
7 Product Technology									
8 Pricing									
9 General Management Skills									
10 Technical Skills									
11 Administrative Skills									
12 End Customer Types	-0.08								
13 Sales Channel Types	0.24**	0.54***							
14 After-sales Services	0.16	0.47***	0.68***						
15 Brand Recognition	0.14	0.27***	0.31***	0.42***					
16 Brand Identity	0.10	0.27***	0.32***	0.48***	0.74***				
17 Supply Channel Types	0.06	0.30***	0.50***	0.51***	0.20**	0.24**			
18 Suppliers	-0.07	0.27***	0.36***	0.40***	0.23**	0.24**	0.73***		
19 Relative Size	0.18*	-0.31***	-0.31***	-0.24**	-0.23**	0.15	-0.22**	-0.15	
20 Speed of Integration	-0.12	-0.02	-0.05	-0.01	0.01	0.00	-0.03	-0.08	-0.03

*** $p < 0.01$, ** $p < 0.05$, * $p < 0.1$

4.3   Multivariate statistics and testing of hypotheses

The survey results and statistical analysis concerning the relationship of business relatedness and synergy realization are presented in this chapter, following the sequence of the hypotheses.

4.3.1 The impact of business relatedness on synergy realization

4.3.1.1   Cost synergy and business relatedness

The initial hypothesis is concerned with the relationship between relatedness and cost synergy. Based on the literature, the following correlation was predicted:

H1: High business relatedness will facilitate cost synergy.

To test the hypothesis, it was determined whether a significant difference existed concerning cost synergy for firms with different degrees of overall relatedness, using an analysis of variance, followed by a multiple regression analysis of the individual factors of relatedness.

The individual factors of relatedness were aggregated to a total score in order to obtain an overall measure of business relatedness. The overall relatedness score was computed using the mean value of the individual factors. The data was subsequently categorized into three groups based on the relatedness score, namely i) low relatedness, ii) medium relatedness and iii) high relatedness. All firms with a relatedness score below the lower 25% percentile were classified into the high relatedness-category, while observations exceeding the upper 25% percentile formed the low relatedness-category. Consequently, the medium relatedness-category consisted of the remaining 50% of the observations with an average degree of relatedness (see table 4-7). The above-mentioned classification appears appropriate since the distribution of the overall relatedness score approximates the normal distribution.

Table 4-7: Classification of business relatedness

High business relatedness (lower 25% percentile)

Factor	n	Mean	SD	Median	Min-Max
Product technology	29	1.9	0.6	1.8	1.0-3.5
End costumers	29	1.6	0.4	1.7	1.0-2.3
General management skills	29	2.5	0.8	2.7	1.0-4.3
Brand recognition	29	2.4	0.8	2.5	1.0-4.0
Supply channels	29	1.8	0.6	2.0	1.0-3.0
Score	29	2.0	0.3	2.1	1.2-2.3

Medium business relatedness

Factor	n	Mean	SD	Median	Min-Max
Product technology	55	2.8	1.0	2.8	1.0-5.0
End costumers	55	2.6	0.8	2.7	1.0-4.7
General management skills	55	3.0	0.8	3.0	1.0-5.0
Brand recognition	54	3.1	0.8	3.0	1.5-5.0
Supply channels	55	3.0	0.9	3.0	1.0-5.0
Score	55	2.9	0.3	2.9	2.4-3.3

Low business relatedness (upper 25% percentile)

Factor	n	Mean	SD	Median	Min-Max
Product technology	26	3.7	0.9	3.5	2.0-5.0
End costumers	26	3.8	0.9	3.8	2.0-5.0
General management skills	25	3.5	0.9	3.3	1.7-5.0
Brand recognition	25	4.1	0.8	4.0	2.0-5.0
Supply channels	26	4.1	0.8	4.3	2.0-5.0
Score	26	3.8	0.5	3.7	3.4-5.0

Note: Business relatedness measured on a five point Likert scale
(1=high relatedness; 5= low relatedness)

Source: Researcher

The relationship between relatedness and cost synergy is illustrated with the help of descriptive statistics. The lowest mean value for cost synergy is achieved by the high relatedness-category. This indicates that cost synergies have been highest for firms with a high degree of relatedness, while the realized cost synergies are lower for firms which exhibit a low degree of relatedness (see table 4-8).

Table 4-8: Dependence of cost synergy on relatedness

Cost synergy

	n	Mean	SD	Median	Min-Max
High relatedness	29	2.45	0.99	2.00	1.00-5.00
Medium relatedness	54	2.83	1.11	2.00	1.00-5.00
Low relatedness	26	3.42	1.10	3.00	2.00-5.00

Note: Cost synergy measured on a five point Likert scale
(1=high cost synergy; 5= low cost synergy)
Source: Researcher

An analysis of variance confirms that there is a significant difference between cost synergy and business relatedness. More specially, the statistical test confirms that firms with a low degree of relatedness are significantly different to the medium and high relatedness categories (see table 4-9).

Table 4-9: Analysis of variance of the dependence of cost synergy on related-ness

	F	p-value
Business relatedness	11.16	0.000
High vs. medium relatedness	2.41	0.124
Medium vs. low relatedness	5.26	0.048
Low vs. high relatedness	11.22	0.003

n=109, Source: Researcher

The multiple regression analysis was conducted using the five factors of business relatedness determined by Pehrsson (2006a) as independent variables. The factors were derived from the survey questionnaire by computing the mean value of the individual items. Missing values were deleted pair-wise to maintain the largest possible sub-sample and to avoid potential bias from mean substitution (Tharenou et al. 2007, p. 205). The reliability of the multi-item measures was tested using Cronbach's coefficient alpha. The alpha values of the five measures ranged between 0.74 and 0.88 and therefore exceeded the generally accepted minimum of 0.70 (Tharenou et al. 2007, p. 153) (see table 4-10).

Table 4-10: Cronbach's Coefficient Alpha

Factor	Cronbach's Alpha
Product Technology	0.88
End Customers	0.79
General Management Skills	0.74
Brand Recognition	0.84
Supply Channels	0.84

Source: Researcher

The model was further tested for multicollinearity using variance inflation factors (Stewart 1987). Typically, variance inflation factors below 10 are deemed to be within an acceptable level (Swaminathan et al. 2008, p. 41). The statistical test revealed that the variance inflation factors ranged between 1.10 and 2.02 which indicates that multicollinearity is not a major concern.

The results of the multiple regression analysis revealed a strong positive and statistically significant relationship between product technology and cost synergy. The data also showed a positive relationship between general management skills and cost synergy, which is however not significant. No independent impact was revealed for the relative size of the merging firms which were controlled for in the model (see table 4-11).

Table 4-11: Multiple regression analysis of relatedness factors on cost synergy

Factor	Coef.	Robust Std. Err.	t	p-value	conf. int (95%)
Product technology	0.37	0.2	2.4	0.018	0.06,0.68
End customers	-0.04	0.1	-0.3	0.766	-0.33,0.25
Gen. Manag. skills	0.22	0.1	1.5	0.142	-0.07,0.52
Brand recognition	0.01	0.1	0.1	0.926	-0.23,0.25
Supply channels	0.04	0.1	0.4	0.705	-0.19,0.28
Relative Size	0.02	0.1	0.3	0.781	-0.14,0.18
Constant	1.01	0.5	2.0	0.048	0.01,2.02
N	102				

adj. R^2 = 0.1074, Source: Researcher

It was therefore concluded that hypothesis H1 was confirmed by the data. A high degree of relatedness will on average facilitate the realization of cost synergy. Based on the multiple regression analysis, it appears that the major underlying drivers of cost synergies are similarities concerning product technology which show a strong positive and significant correlation with the dependent variable.

4.3.1.2   Income synergy and business relatedness

Concerning the relationship between income synergy and business relatedness, hypothesis H2 was formulated: Low business relatedness will facilitate income synergy. A description of the data does not show any material difference in the realized income synergy for the categorized scores of relatedness (see table 4-12).

Table 4-12: Dependence of income synergy on relatedness

Income synergy

	n	Mean	SD	Median	Min-Max
High relatedness	29	2.72	0.96	3.00	1.00-5.00
Medium relatedness	54	2.61	0.79	3.00	1.00-4.00
Low relatedness	26	2.77	1.21	3.00	1.00-5.00

Note: Income synergy measured on a five point Likert scale
(1=high income synergy; 5= low income synergy)
Source: Researcher

Consequently, an analysis of the variance of income synergy's in dependence of business relatedness reveals no statistically significant relationship (p=0.750) (see table 4-13).

Table 4-13: Analysis of variance of the dependence of income synergy on relatedness

	F	p-value
Business relatedness	11.16	0.750

n=109, Source: Researcher

Based on the aggregated score, it was concluded that low relatedness had no positive impact on income synergy. Hypothesis H2 was therefore rejected as unproven by the survey data. However, the multiple regression analysis revealed that a low degree of relatedness concerning supply channels does in fact facilitate the realization of income synergy. This suggests that differences in the purchasing activities of the merging entities prior to the integration can be leveraged and transformed into income synergies (see table 4-14).

Table 4-14: Multiple regression analysis of relatedness factors on income synergy

Factor	Coef.	Robust Std. Err.	t	p-value	conf. int (95%)
Product technology	0.04	0.1	0.3	0.756	-0.19,0.27
End customers	0.15	0.1	1.4	0.167	-0.06,0.37
Gen. Manag. skills	-0.03	0.1	-0.2	0.822	-0.27,0.22
Brand recognition	0.07	0.1	0.6	0.536	-0.16,0.31
Supply channels	-0.24	0.1	-2.1	0.038	-0.46,-0.01
Relative Size	-0.01	0.1	-0.1	0.957	-0.20,0.19
Constant	2.70	0.7	4.1	0.000	1.40,4.00
N	103				

adj. R^2 = 0.0108, Source: Researcher

4.3.1.3   Total synergy and business relatedness

Despite conflicting evidence, there are several studies in the field which suggest that M&A between related parties will generally result in superior performance gains (Lubatkin 1983; Singh and Montgomery 1987; Datta et al. 1992). The academic debate was revisited by testing hypothesis H3: High business relatedness will facilitate total synergy.

A description of the relevant data shows that total synergy is substantially higher for M&A with a high and medium relatedness compared to transactions with a low degree of relatedness (see table 4-15).

Table 4-15: Dependence of total synergy on relatedness

Total Synergy

	n	Mean	SD	Median	Min-Max
High relatedness	28	2.29	0.85	2.00	1.00-5.00
Medium relatedness	55	2.29	0.66	2.00	1.00-4.00
Low relatedness	26	3.12	1.21	3.00	1.00-5.00

Note: Total synergy measured on a five point Likert scale
(1=high total synergy; 5= low total synergy)
Source: Researcher

An analysis of variance confirms that there is a significant difference in the total synergy realization depending on the degree of business relatedness. As already apparent in the description of the data, a statistically significant difference exists between high and medium relatedness on the one hand and low relatedness on the
other hand. No significant difference was observed between the high and medium
relatedness categories (see table 4-16).

**Table 4-16: Analysis of variance of the dependence of total synergy on related-
ness**

	F	p-value
Business relatedness	8.99	0.000
High vs. medium relatedness	0.00	0.980
Medium vs. low relatedness	12.34	0.001
Low vs. high relatedness	15.96	0.000

n=109, Source: Researcher

A multiple regression analysis revealed a positive and statistically significant relationship between product technology and total synergy ($p<0.10$). Furthermore, it
appears that commonalities between the brand recognition of the merging entities
have a positive impact on total synergy. The correlation is however not significant
(see table 4-17).

Table 4-17: Multiple regression analysis of relatedness factors on total synergy

Factor	Coef.	Robust Std. Err.	t	p-value	conf. int (95%)
Product technology	0.23	0.1	1.9	0.061	-0.01,0.46
End customers	0.00	0.1	0.0	0.977	-0.24,0.25
Gen. Manag. skills	-0.03	0.1	-0.2	0.848	-0.29,0.24
Brand recognition	0.16	0.1	1.6	0.120	-0.04,0.36
Supply channels	-0.04	0.1	-0.4	0.666	-0.24,0.15
Relative Size	-0.11	0.1	-1.3	0.185	-0.28,0.05
Constant	1.96	0.5	3.7	0.000	0.90,3.02
N	102				

adj. $R^2 = 0.0857$, Source: Researcher

Based on the statistical tests, it can be concluded that total synergy realization is
more likely to occur for M&A with a high degree of relatedness. The efficiency gains
are primarily attributed to similarities of product technology. Thus, hypothesis H3 is
confirmed by the analysis of survey data.

4.3.1.4   Total synergy and product technology

The literature suggests that similarities concerning product technology have a favourable impact on synergy realization. Accordingly, hypothesis H4 was formulated:
High business relatedness concerning product technology will increase total synergy.

The multiple regression analysis conducted with all factors of relatedness on total
synergy has already provided evidence to support this assumption. However, in
order to test this specific hypothesis, a regression analysis is conducted on product
technology and total synergy which is controlled for the relative size of the merging
entities. The regression analysis reveals a positive and strongly significant relationship between product technology and total synergy ($p<0.01$) (table 4-18). The survey
data therefore provides strong support for the hypothesis.

Table 4-18: Regression analysis of product technology and total synergy

Factor	Coef.	Robust Std. Err.	t	p-value	conf. int (95%)
Product technology	0.27	0.1	2.9	0.004	0.09,0.46
Relative Size	-0.11	0.1	-1.4	0.160	-0.26,0.04
Constant	2.15	0.4	5.0	0.000	1.29,3.00
N	104				

adj. $R^2 = 0.1322$, Source: Researcher

This finding corroborates the result of Pehrsson's study (2006a) who found significant support for the relationship between firm performance and technological relatedness. Based on the multiple regression analyses on income and cost synergy, it
can be concluded that the synergy realization from similarities of product technology
between the merging entities is primarily related to cost economies.

4.3.1.5   Total synergy and resource attributes

The literature suggests that complementary resource patterns between the merging
entities are relevant to the creation of private and unique synergies (Harrison et al.
1991; Hitt et al. 1998). A recent study conducted by Pehrsson (2009) shows that
skills relatedness has a positive impact on foreign subsidiary performance which

lends further support to this notion. Accordingly, the hypothesis H5 is tested: High relatedness concerning resource attributes will increase total synergy.

In line with Pehrsson (2006a), there was a focus on the variable *general management skills* to establish resource relatedness which is measured through three items, namely i) general management skills, ii) technical skills and iii) administrative skills. The measurement approach is basically in line with *skills relatedness* which only includes marketing skills as an additional item to *general management skills* (Pehrsson 2009, p. 40).

A regression analysis on general management skills and total synergy as the dependent variable does not reveal a significant relationship (table 4-19). Similarly, the multiple regression analysis conducted on income and total synergy based on all factors of business relatedness does not yield a significant relationship. The regression analysis on cost synergy shows a positive coefficient for general management skills which is however not statistically significant (p=0.142) (see table 4-11). Therefore, hypothesis H5 is rejected on the basis of the data generated in this study.

Table 4-19: Regression analysis of general management skills and total synergy

Factor	Coef.	Robust Std. Err.	t	p-value	conf. int (95%)
General management skills	0.04	0.1	0.3	0.791	-0.23,0.30
Relative Size	-0.12	0.1	-1.4	0.161	-0.28,0.05
Constant	2.79	0.4	6.3	0.000	1.91,3.68
N	103				

adj. R^2 = 0.0088, Source: Researcher

4.3.1.6   Probability of income and cost synergy realization

Based on the review of the literature, hypothesis H6 was formulated: Overall, cost synergy is more likely to occur than income synergy in M&A. A tabulation of the relevant data shows that a similar number of observations were reported as having *high* and *very high* realizations of income and cost synergy. On the other hand, almost twice as many transactions were reported as having *low* and *very low* cost synergies by comparison to income synergies. This stands in contrast to the hypothesis (see table 4-20).

Table 4-20: Fisher's exact test on income and cost synergy realization

	Income synergy		Cost synergy		p-value
	n	%	n	%	
Very high	9	8.3	7	6.4	0.796
High	41	37.6	44	40.4	0.781
Medium	38	34.9	25	22.9	0.073
Low	18	16.5	22	20.2	0.600
Very low	0	0	11	10.1	0.050

Source: Researcher

The result of Fisher's exact test confirms a significant difference for the category *very low* between income and cost synergy ($p<0.1$). More observations were reported as having a *very low* degree of cost synergy as opposed to income synergy, while no significant difference can be observed for *high* and *very high* income and cost synergy. Hence, hypothesis H6 is rejected on the basis of the survey data.

4.3.2 The impact of speed of integration on synergy realization

Based on the literature, it was expected that a high speed of the M&A integration would be particularly beneficial for transactions with low relatedness between the merging entities. The rationale behind this assumption was that customer uncertainty caused by a merger between firms with different characteristics can be more quickly resolved through a swift realization of the post-merger integration project (Homburg and Bucerius 2006). As such, hypothesis H7 was formulated: Speed of integration will facilitate synergy for M&A with low business relatedness.

The data shows that more than 50 percent of the M&A projects were integrated within 12 months of acquisition. Since there are only a few observations with an integration project beyond 19 months, it was considered appropriate to classify the data into two categories for the purpose of the statistical tests, namely i) higher speed of integration ≤ 12 months (56 observations) and ii) lower speed of integration > 12 months (37 observations). A total number of 14 acquisitions have not been integrated and have therefore been neglected in the following analysis (see table 4-21).

Table 4-21: Speed of post-merger integration project

	n	%
> 24 months	5	4.6
19 - 24 months	7	6.5
13 - 18 months	26	24.1
6 - 12 months	34	31.5
< 6 months	22	20.4
Not integrated	14	13.0
N	108	100.0

Source: Researcher

A tabulation of total synergy in dependence of relatedness and the speed of the integration project reveals a higher extent of synergy realization (1 = very high; 5 = very low) for projects with a comparatively higher speed of integration (≤ 12 months) for all relatedness categories. However, within the subsamples of higher and lower speed of integration, it becomes evident that the achieved synergies are higher for M&A with a high degree of relatedness which contradicts the expected relationship (see table 4-22).

Table 4-22: Dependence of total synergy on relatedness and speed of integration

	n	Mean	SD	Median	Min-Max
Higher speed					
> High relatedness	14	2.00	0.68	2.00	1.00-3.00
> Medium relatedness	27	2.26	0.66	2.00	1.00-4.00
> Low relatedness	15	3.07	1.28	3.00	1.00-5.00
Lower speed					
> High relatedness	11	2.55	1.04	2.00	1.00-5.00
> Medium relatedness	21	2.29	0.64	2.00	1.00-3.00
> Low relatedness	5	3.20	1.30	4.00	1.00-4.00

Note: Higher speed of integration ≤ 12 months, lower speed of integration > 12 months

Source: Researcher

An analysis of variance shows that the speed of the integration project has neither a direct impact on total synergy nor a moderating effect on the relationship between business relatedness and total synergy (see table 4-23).

Table 4-23: Analysis of variance of the dependence of total synergy on related-ness and speed of integration

	F	p-value
Business relatedness	6.07	0.003
Speed of integration	1.28	0.261
Interaction	0.73	0.485

n=93; Source: Researcher

Thus, hypothesis H7 cannot be confirmed by the data.

4.3.3 The planning accuracy and effectiveness of dyssynergy

During the pre-merger stage, corporate executives generally tend to pursue optimistic planning assumptions (Eccles et al. 1999). As a consequence, the literature suggests that acquirers often underestimate the extent of dyssynergies to be incurred during a specific transaction (Early 2004). Hence, hypothesis H8 was formulated: Dyssynergies are on average underestimated in the pre-merger evaluation.

The data reveals that more than 80 percent of the observations reflected low and very low dyssynergies, while only a few M&A transactions have recorded high and very high dyssynergies during the M&A project (see table 4-24).

Table 4-24: Extent of dyssynergy recorded

	n	%
Very low	29	26.6
Low	60	55.0
Medium	14	12.8
High	5	4.6
Very High	1	0.9
N	109	100.0

Source: Researcher

The survey data furthermore shows that the majority of M&A projects did not include an evaluation of the potential dyssynergies during the pre-merger evaluation stage (see table 4-25).

Table 4-25: Consideration of dyssynergies during M&A evaluation

	n	%
Yes	48	44.4
No	60	55.6
N	108	100.0

Source: Researcher

In the subsample of transactions which conducted an evaluation of dyssynergies, more than 85 percent of the transactions either met their dyssynergy targets or managed to reduce the adverse effects below the planned amounts, while only five transactions exceeded their dyssynergy targets. No transaction recorded dyssynergies which were significantly higher than the expectation (see table 4-26).

Table 4-26: Actual dyssynergies compared to expectations

	n	%
Significantly lower	2	4.2
Lower	11	22.9
Met target amount	28	58.3
Higher	5	10.4
Significantly higher	0	0.0
Missing	2	4.2
N	48	100.0

Source: Researcher

Based on the data, it can be concluded that the evaluation of dyssynergies is oftentimes neglected which lends support to the positive bias of acquirers observed in earlier studies (Goold and Campbell 1998). However, for those acquirers which evaluated potential dyssynergies, the expectations were not exceeded. Thus, hypothesis H8 has been rejected.

Based on the literature, it is expected that dyssynergies have a detrimental effect on M&A performance. Therefore, hypothesis H9 was tested: M&A with high dyssynergies are more likely to diminish shareholder value.

Overall M&A performance has been established through shareholder value creation which has been measured on a three point Likert scale with the following items: i) created, ii) preserved and iii) diminished. A crosstabulation of the relevant data reveals that the creation of shareholder value is associated with a comparatively low

extent of dyssynergies, while transactions with a decrease in shareholder value
mostly report high and very high dyssynergies (see table 4-27).

Table 4-27: Crosstabulation of dyssynergy and shareholder value creation

Share holder value	Dyssynergy											
	very high		high		medium		low		very low		Total	
	n	%	n	%	n	%	n	%	n	%	n	%
Created	0	0	0	0	11	84.6	46	78.0	24	82.8	81	75.7
Preserved	0	0	2	40.0	1	7.7	13	22.0	5	17.2	21	19.6
Diminished	1	100	3	60.0	1	7.7	0	0	0	0	5	4.7
N	1	100	5	100	13	100	59	100	29	100	107	100

Source: Researcher

Given that the responses are strongly skewed for both variables, it was decided to
categorize the data. With a total of only 19 observations, the items medium, high and
very high dyssynergy are grouped together into one category. Furthermore, shareholder value creation is reduced to a dichotomous variable by grouping the original
items created and preserved together in order to better discriminate M&A which have
diminished shareholder value from the remaining transactions.

Based on the re-categorized data, Fisher's exact test yields a p-value of 0.000 (see
table 4-28). Hence, the data provides significant support for the relationship between
dyssynergy and shareholder value creation; that is, the higher the degree of dyssynergy recorded, the higher the likelihood that the transaction will diminish shareholder
value. As a result, hypothesis H9 can be confirmed based on the survey data.

Table 4-28: Re-categorized crosstabulation of dyssynergy and shareholder value

Shareholder value	Dyssynergy							
	very high-medium		low		very low		Total	
	n	%	n	%	n	%	n	%
Diminished	5	26.3	0	0	0	0	5	4.7
Created/preserved	14	73.7	59	100.0	29	100.0	102	95.3
N	19	100.0	59	100.0	29	100.0	107	100.0

Source: Researcher

4.3.4 M&A category and shareholder value creation

Academics have extensively researched the impact of diversification on firm performance (Prahalad and Bettis 1986). Based on the conventional wisdom, M&A
between related firms are viewed more favourably in terms of value creation than
conglomerate transactions (Datta et al. 1992). Accordingly, hypothesis H10 was
tested: Horizontal M&A create more shareholder value for the shareholders of the
acquiring firm than diversification-based M&A. For the purpose of the statistical tests,
it was decided to use the FTC classification which provides an objective and readily
available classification of merger relatedness (Lubatkin 1987, p. 41). Moreover, the
FTC classification provides an additional measure of relatedness to reveal any inconsistencies in the multi-dimensional measurement approach applied in this study.
A comparison of the two measures of relatedness shows that horizontal M&A on
average exhibit a higher degree of similarities than conglomerate transactions which
provides support for the validity of the multi-dimensional conceptualization of relatedness (see appendix 2).

A description of the data illustrates that the majority of acquirers have pursued horizontal M&A, while less than 15 percent of the observations constitute conglomerate
transactions (see table 4-4). A crosstabulation of the data does not reveal any no-
ticeable difference between the M&A category and shareholder value creation (see
table 4-29). Fisher's exact test reports a p-value of 0.444 which confirms that there is
no statistically significant relationship between M&A category and shareholder value
creation. Thus, hypothesis 10 has been rejected by the data.

Table 4-29: Crosstabulation of M&A category and shareholder value creation

Shareholder Value	M & A							
	Horizontal / Horizontal with market exten- sion		Horizontal with product exten- sion		Vertical		Conglomerate / Diversification	
	n	%	n	%	n	%	n	%
Diminished	1	2.4	3	7.9	1	7.7	0	0
Created/preserved	41	97.6	35	92.1	12	92.3	15	100.0
N	42	100.0	38	100.0	13	100.0	15	100.0

Source: Researcher

4.3.5 The effectiveness of relative size

Previous research projects have observed a size effect in the context of M&A. It is argued that a substantial relative size of the target firm compared to the acquiring firm is a prerequisite to realize significant performance gains (Chatterjee 1986; Seth 1990). In other words, M&A are more likely to diminish value and result in a failure in the case of a size mismatch (Kitching 1967). Accordingly, the relative size of the merging entities has been controlled in this study.

Table 4-30: Relative size of target firm compared to acquiring firm

	n	%
>100 %	8	7.6
75-100%	6	5.7
50-74%	9	8.6
25-49%	13	12.4
<25%	69	65.7
N	105	100.0

Source: Researcher

A frequency distribution of the survey data shows that more than 75 percent of the target firms have reported less than 50 percent of the revenue of the acquiring firm prior to the M&A transaction (see table 4-30). The correlation matrix reveals that relative size has a significant negative correlation with total synergy (see table 4-6). This suggests that total synergy is lower for those transactions with a comparatively higher relative size of acquiring firm to target firm. However, the statistical significance of the simple linear regression might be influenced by the distribution of relative size which is strongly skewed towards small target firms with a mean value of 4.23 on a five point Likert scale (1 = ">100%"; 5 = "<25%"). The multiple regression analyses conducted on total, income and cost synergy do not reveal any significant relationship for relative size. Hence, it can be concluded that the survey data does not exhibit a size effect.

4.4   Discussion of research findings

The survey results provide evidence that business relatedness has a statistically significant impact on the realization of synergy. The extent of total synergy has been substantially higher for M&A with a medium and high degree of relatedness as opposed to transactions with a low degree of relatedness. The synergy realization is largely contingent on similarities concerning product technology which have revealed a positive and statistically significant correlation with total synergy achievement. This finding suggests that performance gains are primarily achieved in the area of production. In related acquisitions, it is possible to realize economies of scale and scope through sharing of resources and joint production, while performance gains in unrelated acquisitions are limited to general efficiencies in the area of administration as well as from reduced financing cost (Singh and Montgomery 1987, p. 379).

A significant positive relationship was revealed between technological relatedness and total synergy realization, corroborating the finding of Pehrsson (2006a) who observed higher profitability for diversified firms with similar product technology. The researcher argues that the performance gains are attributed to the accumulated competence in a technological field which conditions returns to investments in a similar field. Hence, performance gains are expected to be higher in areas which are related to the firm's established competence (Pehrsson 2006a, p. 275). The finding that synergistic gains have been higher for M&A with related product technology might furthermore be associated with the inflexible nature of physical resources which are only useful in a very few similar industries. This implies that any excess capacity of physical resources is unlikely to be used efficiently in conglomerate M&A outside the firm's core business (Chatterjee and Wernerfelt 1991a, p. 35). In contrast to the expectations, the survey data does not support the hypothesis that high relatedness concerning resource attributes will facilitate synergy realization. According to Pehrsson (2009), the positive performance effects observed for foreign subsidiaries with high skills relatedness are primarily attributed to economies of learning. In the context of the present study, it was speculated that the majority of M&A have not been pursued with the explicit intent to reap economies from learning, being a possible explanation why synergistic gains have not been observed for transactions with high skills relatedness. Furthermore, the lack of support for the relationship between synergy realization and high relatedness of resource attributes might be attributed to the measurement approach which did not consider the relatedness of marketing skills as was the case in Pehrsson's (2009) study. Previous contributions in the field advocate that the combination of marketing resources is particularly suitable to generate synergistic benefits (Larsson and Finkelstein 1999; Swaminathan et al. 2008).

In line with the expectations, the survey data show that a high degree of relatedness facilitates the realization of cost synergy. Based on the multiple regression analysis, it becomes apparent that the efficiency gains are attributed to similar product technology between the merging firms. This finding lends support to the argument of Swaminathan (2008) who revealed that similar resource patterns facilitate performance gains in consolidation-based mergers which are pursued with the primary objective to realize cost efficiencies. Similar resources allow the management of the merged entity to exploit cost efficiencies from a reduction of excess capacity, the leveraging of pre-existing resources and critical success factors as well as to realize learning curve effects. Conversely, M&A which exhibit different resource patterns between acquiring and target firm are more likely to suffer from cultural clashes and disadvantages of combining dissimilar resources (Swaminathan et al. 2008, p. 38).

Based on the literature, it was furthermore expected that a low degree of relatedness will facilitate income synergy since differences in the resource allocations will complement the merging entities. Value gains would be expected through the transfer and application of resources in alternative processes, especially if excess resources are matched to resource deficiencies in a particular value chain activity (Swaminathan et al. 2008, p. 38). The data however does not provide any support for the hypothesis that differences between the merging firms in general will facilitate income synergy. It was however found that differences in the configuration of the supply channels are in fact associated with the realization of income synergy. This finding suggests that deficiencies in certain input factors can be addressed through the merger of a firm which controls different suppliers and supply channel types. The finding that an overall low degree of relatedness does not facilitate income synergy might be related to complementarities between the merging entities being a prerequisite to realize efficiency gains. Hitt et al. (1998) revealed that complementary of assets and resources are an important condition to achieving positive synergy and sustainable competitive advantage. However, the degree of relatedness does not necessarily reflect the complementarity of resources being a possible explanation for the fact that no significant difference was observed between overall relatedness and income synergy (Hitt et al. 1998, p. 107). Furthermore, the study focussed on operating synergies, while deliberately neglecting financial synergies which are commonly associated with diversification-based M&A between unrelated entities (Trautwein 1990, p. 284). Hence, any financial synergies accomplished through complementary resources have not been captured by the research design.

Based on the extant literature, there is strong evidence that cost synergy is more likely to occur than income synergy (KPMG 1999; Pautler 2003; Early 2004). The survey data did however not confirm this notion. Instead, weak support was found for a low degree of cost synergy being more likely to occur than low income synergy. A possible explanation for the unexpected high degree of income synergy could be related to most of the M&A included in the survey having been in pursuit of revenue enhancement through cross-selling and access to new geographic markets. The majority of the observations (56%) constituted cross-border transactions which lends some support for this explanation. Moreover, it has to be appreciated that the survey results are based on the perceptions of M&A consultants. It can therefore not be ruled out that the evaluation of the respondents is free from positive bias (Pautler 2003, p. 4).

The relationship between the speed of the integration project and synergy realization has been evaluated. Based on the literature, it was expected that a swift integration would be particularly beneficial for merging entities with a low degree of relatedness (Homburg and Bucerius 2006). The rationale behind the hypothesis is that customer uncertainty with potentially adverse performance effects can be more quickly resolved through a timely integration. The survey data does however not provide any statistically significant support for this relationship. A possible explanation for the lack of support might be associated with the internal relatedness between the merging entities being not considered in the research project. Based on the study conducted by Homburg and Bucerius (2006), strong evidence was found that high speed of the integration project is beneficial for low external relatedness while being detrimental for M&A with a low degree of internal relatedness. The researchers argue that low internal relatedness, which encompasses management styles, pre-merger performance and strategic orientation, is frequently associated with employee resistance, internal turbulence and reduced employee retention. Hence, a quick integration of firms with low internal relatedness is more likely to result in internal conflicts, particular from divergent organizational cultures. The literature provides ample evidence that cultural differences have the potential to cause major detrimental effects on the post-merger performance (Chatterjee et al. 1992; Badrtalei and Bates 2007).

Previous contributions in the field have suggested that adverse effects associated with M&A are oftentimes neglected (Goold and Campbell 1998; Eccles et al. 1999; Early 2004). The data did not support the hypothesis that dyssynergies are on average underrated during the pre-merger evaluation. In fact, only about 10 percent of the transactions reported dyssynergies which have exceeded the planned values. However, the survey results also revealed that the majority of acquirers did not specifically consider dyssynergies during the pre-merger evaluation. This finding clearly illustrates that many acquirers do not appreciate the relevance of dyssynergy for the M&A evaluation. This observation is particularly surprising given the strong statistical support provided by the survey data that dyssynergy has an adverse impact on shareholder value creation.

Lastly, the study has evaluated the impact of the M&A category on shareholder value creation. Based on the literature, it was expected that horizontal M&A created more shareholder value for the acquiring firm than diversification-based transactions due to the opportunity to establish linkages between the value chains (Ensign 1998). The survey results do not provide any evidence for the hypothesis. This lends further support to recent contributions rejecting the notion that conglomerate M&A suffer from inferior performance gains on the grounds that selectivity bias has not been considered in earlier studies (Campa and Kedia 2002; Villalonga 2004). The finding that horizontal and conglomerate M&A perform equally well in terms of shareholder wealth creation might be related to differences in the benefits that accrue to diversification-based transactions. Linkages between the merging entities with the objective to realize operating synergy might be more difficult to establish in conglomerate M&A. Instead, conglomerate M&A target financial synergies, risk diversification and increased flexibility. A survey with financial executives reveals that diversification is a justifiable merger motive which supports the notion that the value potential in conglomerate M&A is equal to horizontal transactions (Mukherjee et al. 2004, p. 18).

Based on the literature, it was expected that relative size would have a positive moderating impact on synergy realization (Chatterjee 1986; Seth 1990). The survey data did not support the hypothesis. Instead, the correlation matrix shows a negative correlation between relative size and total synergy realization which might be related to the primarily small and medium-sized enterprises which were included in the survey. As shown earlier, the average size of the acquiring firms is significantly lower than in other research projects in the field. The survey has been conducted with IMAP which is an organization of M&A consultants being specialized in medium-sized transactions. It can be speculated that medium-sized acquirers have less management resources at their disposal which renders synergy realization in their larger acquisitions more difficult to accomplish.

4.5   Limitations

The study is subject to several limitations. The first limitation is related to the research design which is based on a survey of M&A consultants. Surveys with executives are often criticized for a lack of objectivity and positive bias (Bruner 2002, p. 51). The argument of Walter and Barney (1990) however provides support that a survey with M&A consultants is less prone to response bias than studies conducted with corporate executives.

> First, the executives of an acquiring firm have a strong incentive to make it appear that their actions are consistent with the shareholder's interest. Also, to justify their own actions, executives may be unwilling to discuss the original goals or objectives for a merger or acquisition that has not met those goals or objectives. While not free from these biases, it was felt that data from professional intermediaries would be less affected. Second, while company executives may understand their own goals or objectives, their experience tends to be company- or industry-specific. By contrast, intermediaries have a broader

experience base from which to draw in making the judgements elicited here (Walter and Barney 1990, p. 79).

Second, the research design was confined to explore the impact of similarities and differences concerning key attributes of the merging entities on synergy realization. However, empirical evidence suggests that complementarities are equally important to explain M&A performance (Harrison et al. 1991; Hitt et al. 1998; Larsson and Finkelstein 1999). As argued by Larsson and Finkelstein (1999, p. 15) "[...] 'economies of fitness' arising from complementary operations – and not just 'economies of sameness' arising from similar operations – are important components of what makes acquisitions work". Based on the research design adopted in this study, performance effects which are attributed to complementarities have not been captured.

Third, it has to be appreciated that the research into firm performance using a multi-dimensional conceptualization of business relatedness based on managerial perceptions is still evolving. Further investigations are required to better understand the individual factors of business relatedness, in particular in the context of M&A.

Last, it has to be emphasized that M&A performance is influenced by a multitude of factors (Datta et al. 1992; Bruner 2004; Christofferson et al. 2004). While the researcher has made an effort to account for the most relevant variables, it cannot be ruled out that other factors have influenced the research findings.

5 Summary and implications of research findings

The impact of relatedness on M&A performance has been extensively researched for the last few decades (Lubatkin 1987; Chatterjee and Wernerfelt 1991a; Hitt et al. 1998). Despite conflicting evidence, the relevant literature suggests that similarities between the merging entities generally facilitate performance gains (Lubatkin 1983; Singh and Montgomery 1987; Datta et al. 1992).

Scholars active in the field argue that the inconsistent findings are partly attributed to weakness in the measurement approach (Sirower 1997). Recent contributions there-fore suggest conceptualizing business relatedness as a multi-dimensional construct (Stimpert and Duhaime 1997; Pehrsson 2006a; Pehrsson 2006b). Therefore, it was decided to adopt the measurement approach of Pehrsson (2006a) who captured business relatedness as a multi-dimensional concept based on managerial percep-tions. The measurement approach, which in previous studies has only been applied to explore the performance implications to diversified firms (Pehrsson 2006a; Pehrsson 2009), has been transferred to the field of M&A with the objective to shed further light on the impact of relatedness on synergy realization.

Recent research suggests that the impact of relatedness is contingent on the merger motive (Swaminathan et al. 2008). A high degree of similarity concerning the configuration of resource patterns between the merging firms has been found to be more favourable to consolidation-driven M&A with the objective to realize cost re-ductions, while a low degree of relatedness is considered beneficial for conglomerate M&A targeting new revenue streams from the combination of complementary re-sources. Hence, in contrast to earlier studies, which have primarily focused on the overall M&A performance using accounting or stock-market data (Chatterjee 1986; Lubatkin 1987; Singh and Montgomery 1987), it was decided to explore the impact of relatedness on income and cost economies in addition to the total synergy realiza-tion. Moreover, the adverse impact of dyssynergies on M&A performance had been emphasized in recent research contributions (Early 2004; Hofmann 2004; Lechner

2007a). It was therefore decided to investigate the effectiveness of dyssynergy and the extent to which negative synergy is reflected during the pre-merger evaluation.

Besides, it has been examined in this study in how far the speed of the integration project will influence the realization of synergy. The research findings of the study conducted by Homburg and Bucerius (2006) suggest that a swift post-merger integration project is particularly beneficial for M&A between firms with a low degree of relatedness.

5.1   Summary of key research findings

The study provides further support to the common notion that relatedness facilitates synergy realization in M&A. However, a high degree of relatedness has only been found to be beneficial for the realization of cost synergy, while no significant difference could be observed for income synergy.

Hence, the study provides further evidence that the impact of relatedness is largely contingent on the M&A motive (Swaminathan et al. 2008). High relatedness between the merging firms is particularly favourable for consolidation-based acquisitions with the objective to realize cost efficiencies. The research project thus lends further support to Chatterjee's proposition that horizontal M&A with the intent to realize cost synergy are most likely to succeed (Chatterjee 2007, p. 49).

The underlying driver to realize synergy in related M&A is the similarity of the product technology of the merging firms. In acquisitions with high technological relatedness, it is therefore possible to capture economies of scale and scope from sharing of resources and joint production, while performance gains in unrelated M&A are confined to general efficiency gains in the area of administration and financing (Singh and Montgomery 1987). The study thus corroborates the research finding of Pehrsson (2006a) who observed significantly higher performance levels for diversified firms with technological relatedness between the business units. It therefore appears that the product technology reflects the core competence of a firm which allows the exploitation of operating synergies (Pehrsson 2006a, p. 275).

It was furthermore found that low relatedness concerning the configuration of the supply channels will facilitate income synergy. This suggests that deficiencies concerning input factors can be addressed by the acquisition of a target firm with different suppliers and supply channel types. No statistically significant support was found for the idea that low relatedness in general will facilitate income synergy. Moreover, the study failed to provide evidence that high relatedness concerning resource attributes will in general facilitate synergy.

Based on the literature, it was expected that cost synergy was more likely to occur than income synergy (Pautler 2003; Early 2004). The data did not confirm this hypothesis; instead, weak support was found that income synergy is easier to accomplish. As the majority of the M&A constitute cross-border M&A, it can be speculated that most of the transactions considered in the survey have been realized with the intent to accomplish income synergy from cross-selling and access to new geographical markets.

The survey data did not confirm the hypothesis that high speed of the post-merger integration project will be particularly favourable for M&A with low relatedness. The lack of support is likely to be associated with the fact that the internal relatedness between the merging firms, in particular differences in the organizational cultures, was not considered. Based on the survey design, which was confined to external relatedness, the speed of integration has shown neither a direct nor a moderating effect on synergy realization.

The study has furthermore revealed that the majority of acquirers do not explicitly consider dyssynergy during the pre-merger evaluation. The survey data confirms the hypothesis that dyssynergy has a strong negative correlation with shareholder value creation.

The study did not provide any evidence that the M&A category has a significant impact on M&A performance. This finding therefore provides further support to recent contributions which advocate that horizontal and conglomerate M&A in general

Table 5-1: Summary of research findings

Research Question	Hypothesis	Statistical Test	Key observations
1. To what extent does business relatedness impact synergy in M&A?	H1: High business relatedness will facilitate cost synergy.	Confirmed	Major driver of cost synergy is similarity of product technology.
	H2: Low business relatedness will facilitate income synergy.	Rejected	Overall hypothesis rejected, however significant support has been found for low relatedness concerning supply channels facilitating income synergy.
	H3: High business relatedness will facilitate total synergy.	Confirmed	Major driver of total synergy is similarity of product technology.
	H4: High business relatedness concerning product technology will increase total synergy.	Confirmed	Strong support has been found for similar product technology facilitating total synergy.
	H5: High relatedness concerning resource attributes will increase total synergy.	Rejected	No support has been found for the relationship between general management skills and total synergy.
	H6: Overall, cost synergy is more likely to occur than income synergy in M&A.	Rejected	Weak support has been found for income synergy being easier to generate than cost synergy.
2. To what extent does the speed of the post-merger	H7: Speed of integration will facilitate synergy for	Rejected	Speed of integration has neither a direct nor a mod-

Research Question	Hypothesis	Statistical Test	Key observations
integration project influence synergy realization?	M&A with low business related-ness.		erating effect on synergy realization.
3. What is the planning accuracy and effectiveness of dyssynergy?	H8: Dyssynergies are generally un-derestimated in the pre-merger evaluation.	Rejected	Majority of acquir-ers do not evaluate dyssynergies. If considered, actual dyssynergy mostly remains within the planned range.
	H9: M&A with high dyssynergies are more likely to di-minish shareholder value.	Confirmed	Strong statistical support for the hypothesis, how-ever only a few observations report diminished share-holder value.
4. What is the impact of diversifi-cation on M&A performance?	H10: Horizontal M&A create more shareholder value for the sharehold-ers of the acquiring firm than diversifi-cation-based M&A.	Rejected	No support has been found to support the hy-pothesis. Most acquirers have pursued horizontal M&A.

Source: Researcher

perform equally well in terms of shareholder wealth creation (Campa and Kedia 2002; Villalonga 2004).

A size effect, which has been observed in previous research projects (Chatterjee 1986; Seth 1990), could not be found in the subject study which is probably related to the majority of the transactions having been conducted by medium-sized compa-nies, which have limited resources at their disposal to acquire and successfully inte-grate large target firms.

The key findings of the research project are summarized in table 5-1.

5.2   Implications for theory and practice

The research project has shed new light on the academic debate on the perform-ance implications of relatedness. In contrast to earlier studies, the impact of business relatedness on M&A performance has been investigated separately for cost and income economies. The study provides strong empirical evidence that a high degree of relatedness is particularly beneficial for the realization of cost synergies. The ma-jor underlying driver to yield cost economies are similarities in the product technology of the merging firms. The degree of relatedness has no predictive power to explain income synergy in general, yet differences in the supply channels appear to be fa-vourable to enhanced revenue streams. The study thus provides an explanation for the conflicting evidence on the impact of relatedness on M&A performance in prior research projects which have investigated overall performance gains without consid-eration of cost and income economies. The study has furthermore shown that the predictive power varies significantly amongst the individual factors of relatedness which lends further support to the recent stream of research advocating a multi-di-mensional conceptualization of business relatedness (Stimpert and Duhaime 1997; Pehrsson 2006a; Pehrsson 2006b).

The research findings provide important implications for practitioners. Most notably, the study shows that the degree of relatedness enables the management of the acquiring firm to better anticipate the synergistic potential for a specific target. This finding is particularly relevant given that synergy is often used to justify high acquisi-tion premiums (Kode et al. 2003). Empirical evidence shows that there is a signifi-cant negative correlation between the acquisition premium and M&A performance (Sirower 1997). The negative performance impact of the acquisition premium is likely to be aggravated if the pre-merger evaluation and purchase price considerations are based on overrated assumptions concerning the synergistic potential. Specifically, the study has shown that the synergistic potential is highest for M&A with technologi-cal relatedness pursued with the intent to realize cost economies. During the pre-merger evaluation, it is therefore advisable to conduct plausibility checks bearing in mind the merger motive and the degree of relatedness as well as to evaluate the necessary revenue and cost synergies required to recover the premium as proposed by Sirower and Sahni (2006).

When evaluating projected synergies, setting reasonable thresholds above which successful cost reduction and revenue improvement become implausible is critical in assessing the extent of the operating challenge associated with any deal being contemplated (Sirower and Sahni 2006, p. 90).

Moreover, the study has revealed that the majority of acquiring firms neglect the consideration of dyssynergies during the pre-merger evaluation. This finding is surprising given that M&A with a high degree of dyssynergy are more likely to diminish shareholder value. It is therefore recommended that acquirers evaluate dyssynergy including the cost of establishing value chain linkage required for the sharing of skills and resources in conjunction with the corresponding cost and income synergy (Shaver 2006; Lechner 2007b; Lechner 2007a).

5.3 Suggestions for future research

The study has investigated the impact of relatedness on M&A performance based on various dimensions using managerial perceptions. The measurement approach has only been developed in the recent past in order to address the criticism of established measures of relatedness (Stimpert and Duhaime 1997; Pehrsson 2006a; Pehrsson 2006b). Further research is therefore required to establish the construct validity as well as to verify the individual dimensions of relatedness.

The research project has examined the performance implication of similarities concerning product/market, resource and supply channel attributes of the merging firms. Prior studies however argue that complementarities are equally relevant to explain value creation in M&A (Harrison et al. 1991; Hitt et al. 1998; Larsson and Finkelstein 1999). It is therefore suggested that there be further exploration of the effectiveness of similarities and complementarities on synergy realization to better understand the phenomena of "economies of fitness" and "economies of sameness" (Larsson and Finkelstein 1999, p. 15).

The study failed to confirm earlier research findings indicating a high degree of relatedness concerning resource attributes to facilitate overall synergy realization (Pehrsson 2009). The author argues that synergy from skills relatedness is primarily related to economies of learning. It appears necessary to better understand the underlying mechanisms and prerequisites to accomplish synergy from resource attributes for varying degrees of similarity and/or complementarity.

The measurement approach, which is using managerial perceptions in order to establish the degree of relatedness, has been transferred from the diversification research to the field of M&A. The research project therefore requires repetition in order to test for the stability of the results. Such efforts might use a different sample, such as corporate practitioners.

Appendices

Appendix 1: Research Instrument

A. Personal Information

1. What is your current position? *(Please check only one box or fill in.)*

Managing Partner ☐ Partner ☐

Manager ☐ Associate ☐

Other: _____

B. Information on Acquiring Firm

2. Please indicate the industry affiliation of the acquiring firm? *(Please check only one box or fill in.)*

Agriculture, forestry and fishing	☐	Information and communication	☐
Mining and quarrying	☐	Financial insurance activities	☐
Manufacturing	☐	Real estate activities	☐
Electricity, gas, steam and air conditioning	☐	Professional, scientific and technical services	☐
Water supply; sewerage, waste and remediation activities	☐	Administrative and support services	☐
Wholesales and retail trade; repair of motor vehicles	☐	Public administration and defence	☐
Transportation and storage	☐	Education	☐
Arts, entertainment and social work	☐	Human health and social work	☐
Accommodation and food services	☐	Construction	☐

Other: _____
           Please specify!

3. Please specify the annual turnover of the acquiring firm for last financial year. *(Please fill in.)*

Turnover: _____m EUR

4. Please specify the number employees of the acquiring firm. *(Please fill in.)*

Number of employees: _____

5. Please specify the country of the registered head office of the acquiring firm *(Please fill in.)*

Head Office: _____

D. Information on M&A Project

6. Is the M&A project a domestic or cross-border transaction involving an entity which is not registered in the same country as the acquiring firm? *(Please check only one box.)*

Domestic   ☐

Cross-border   ☐

7. How do you best classify the M&A project? *(Please check only one box.)*

Horizontal   ☐   Horizontal with product extension   ☐

Vertical   ☐   Conglomerate / Diversification   ☐

8. Please indicate the similarity of the key activities of the merging firms with regards to the following attributes? *(Please check only one box per attribute.)*

	Very Similar	Similar	Medium	Different	Very Different
I. Product-Market Attributes					
a. Product Use	☐	☐	☐	☐	☐
b. End Customer Types	☐	☐	☐	☐	☐
c. Product Design	☐	☐	☐	☐	☐
d. Product Technology	☐	☐	☐	☐	☐
e. Pricing	☐	☐	☐	☐	☐

	Very Similar	Similar	Medium	Different	Very Different
II. Resource Attributes					
f. **General Management Skills**	☐	☐	☐	☐	☐
g. **Technical Skills**	☐	☐	☐	☐	☐
h. **Administrative Skills**	☐	☐	☐	☐	☐
i. **Brand Identity**	☐	☐	☐	☐	☐
j. **Brand Recognition**	☐	☐	☐	☐	☐

	Very Similar	Similar	Medium	Different	Very Different
III. Value Chain Attributes					
k. **Sales Channel Types**	☐	☐	☐	☐	☐
l. **After-sales Services**	☐	☐	☐	☐	☐
m. **Supply Channel Types**	☐	☐	☐	☐	☐
n. **Suppliers**	☐	☐	☐	☐	☐

9. Please estimate the amount of total synergies achieved in the M&A project. *(Please check only one box.)*

	Very High	High	Medium	Low	Very Low
Total Synergy	☐	☐	☐	☐	☐

10. More specifically, please estimate the amount of the following synergistic effects achieved in the M&A project. *(Please check only one box per synergistic effect.)*

	Very High	High	Medium	Low	Very Low
a. Income Synergy	☐	☐	☐	☐	☐
b. Cost Synergy	☐	☐	☐	☐	☐

11. Has the M&A project met the planned income and cost synergies? *(Please check only one box per synergistic effect.)*

	Failed Significantly	Failed	Met	Exceeded	Exceeded Significantly
a. Income Synergy	☐	☐	☐	☐	☐
b. Cost Synergy	☐	☐	☐	☐	☐

12. Please estimate the amount of dyssynergies incurred in the M&A project. *(Please check only one box.)*

	Very High	High	Medium	Low	Very Low
Dyssynergy	☐	☐	☐	☐	☐

13a. Have dyssynergies been considered in the M&A evaluation? *(Please check only one box.)*

Yes   ☐

No   ☐

13b. If yes, how do the actual dyssynergies compare to the planned amounts? *(Please check only one box.)*

	Significantly lower	Lower	Met target amounts	Higher	Significantly higher
Dyssynergy	☐	☐	☐	☐	☐

14. Overall, did the M&A project create value for the shareholders of the acquiring company? *(Please check only one box.)*

a. Created Shareholder Value   ☐

b. Preserved Shareholder Value   ☐

c. Destroyed Shareholder Value   ☐

15. Please specify the relative size of the acquisition target to the acquirer in terms of revenue? *(Please check only one box.)*

	>100%	75-100%	50-74%	25-49%	<25%
Relative Size	☐	☐	☐	☐	☐

16. Please indicate the time it has taken to complete the post-merger integration from the date of closing. *(Please check only one box.)*

a. Less than 6 months   ☐

b. 6-12 months   ☐

c. 13-18 months   ☐

d. 19-24 months   ☐

e. More than 24 months   ☐

f. Entities have not been integrated   ☐

Appendix 2: Description of FTC merger classification and business relatedness

Product technology

	N	Mean	SD	Median	Min-Max
Horizon. with market ext.	43	2.2	0.8	2.0	1.0-4.8
Horizon. with product ext.	38	2.9	0.8	2.8	1.5-5.0
Vertical	13	3.3	1.3	3.3	1.0-5.0
Conglomerate	16	3.6	1.3	4.0	1.0-5.0

End customers

	N	Mean	SD	Median	Min-Max
Horizon. with market ext.	43	2.1	0.8	2.0	1.0-4.0
Horizon. with product ext.	38	2.7	0.8	2.7	1.3-5.0
Vertical	13	3.1	1.2	3.0	1.0-5.0
Conglomerate	16	3.4	1.4	3.8	1.0-5.0

General management skills

	N	Mean	SD	Median	Min-Max
Horizon. with market ext.	43	2.9	0.9	3.0	1.0-5.0
Horizon. with product ext.	38	3.0	0.9	3.0	1.0-5.0
Vertical	12	2.8	0.7	2.7	2.0-4.3
Conglomerate	16	3.0	1.0	3.0	1.0-5.0

Brand recognition

	N	Mean	SD	Median	Min-Max
Horizon. with market ext.	42	3.1	1.0	3.0	1.0-5.0
Horizon. with product ext.	38	3.0	0.9	3.0	1.5-5.0
Vertical	12	3.0	1.1	3.0	1.0-4.0
Conglomerate	16	3.4	1.1	3.5	2.0-5.0

Supply channels

	N	Mean	SD	Median	Min-Max
Horizon. with market ext.	43	2.5	1.1	2.5	1.0-5.0
Horizon. with product ext.	38	2.8	0.9	3.0	1.0-4.5
Vertical	13	3.6	1.2	4.0	1.0-5.0
Conglomerate	16	3.8	1.1	4.0	2.0-5.0

Source: Researcher

References

Ansoff, H I 1965, *Corporate Strategy - An Analytic Approach to Business Policy for Growth and Expansion*, London, 1965.

Badrtalei, J and Bates, D L 2007, 'Effect of Organizational Cultures on Mergers and Acquisitions: The Case of Daimler Chrysler', *International Journal of Management*, Vol. 24, No. 2, pp. 303-317.

Bamberger, B 1994, *Der Erfolg von Unternehmensakquisitionen in Deutschland: Eine theoretische und empirische Untersuchung*, University Bamberg, PhD Thesis, pp. 395

Barney, J 1991, 'Firm Resources and Sustained Competitive Advantage', *Journal of Management*, Vol. 17, No. 1, pp. 99-120.

Bass, F M, Cattin, P and Wittink, D R 1978, 'Firm Effects and Industry Effects in the Analysis of Market Structure and Profitability', *Journal of Marketing Research*, Vol. 15, No. 1, pp. 3-10.

Berkovitch, E and Narayanan, M P 1993, 'Motives for Takeovers: An Empirical Investigation', *Journal of Financial & Quantitative Analysis*, Vol. 28, No. 3, pp. 347-362.

Bertoncel, A 2006, 'Acquisition Valuation: How to Value a Going Concern?' *Nase Gospodarstvo/Our Economy*, Vol. 52, No. 5-6, pp. 116-125.

Bruner, R 2004, 'Where M&A Pays and Where It Strays: A Survey of the Research', *Journal of Applied Corporate Finance*, Vol. 16, No. 4, pp. 63-76.

Bruner, R F 2002, 'Does M&A Pay? A Survey of Evidence for the Decision-Maker', *Journal of Applied Finance*, Vol. 12, No. 1, pp. 48-68.

Campa, J M and Kedia, S 2002, 'Explaining the Diversification Discount', *Journal of Finance*, Vol. 57, No. 4, pp. 1731-1762.

Campbell, A, Goold, M and Alexander, M 1995, 'The value of the parent company', *California Management Review*, Vol. 38, No. 1, pp. 79-97.

Carmines, E and Zeller, R 1979, *Reliability and Validity Assessment (Quantitative Applications in the Social Sciences)* Ohio, Sage.

Cavana, R Y, Delahaye, B L and Sekaran, U 2001, *Applied Business Research: Qualitative and Quantitative Methods*, New York, John Wiley & Sons.

Chatterjee, S 1986, 'Types of Synergy and Economic Value: The Impact of Acquisitions on Merging and Rival Firms', *Strategic Management Journal*, Vol. 7, No. 2, pp. 119-139.

Chatterjee, S 1992, 'Sources of Value in Takeovers: Synergy or Restructuring - Implications for Target and Bidder Firms', *Strategic Management Journal*, Vol. 13, No. 4, pp. 267-286.

Chatterjee, S 2007, 'Why is Synergy so Difficult in Mergers of Related Businesses?' *Strategy & Leadership*, Vol. 35, No. 2, pp. 46-52.

Chatterjee, S, Lubatkin, M H, Schweiger, D M and Weber, Y 1992, 'Cultural Differences and Shareholder Value in Related Mergers: Linking Equity and Human Capital ', *Strategic Management Journal*, Vol. 13, No. 5, pp. 319-334.

Chatterjee, S and Wernerfelt, B 1991a, 'The Link between Resources and Type of Diversification: Theory and Evidence', *Strategic Management Journal*, Vol. 12, No. 1, pp. 33-48.

Chatterjee, S and Wernerfelt, B 1991b, *Related or Unrelated Diversification: A Resource Based Approach*. Academy of Management Proceedings, Academy of Management, August 1988, pp. 7-11.

Christofferson, S A, McNish, R S and Sias, D L 2004, 'Where Mergers Go Wrong', *McKinsey Quarterly*, No. 2, pp. 92-99.

Cohen, J, Cohen, P, West, S and Aiken, L 2003, *Applied Multiple Regression /Correlation Analysis for the Behavioral Sciences*, Mahwah, New Jersey, Lawrence Erlbaum Associates.

Federal Trade Commission 1981, *Statistical Report on Mergers and Acquisitions 1978,* U. S. G. P. Office, Washington D.C.

Cronbach, L 1951, 'Coefficient Alpha and The Internal Structure of Tests', *Psychometrika*, Vol. 16, pp. 297-334.

Datta, D K, Pinches, G E and Narayanan, V K 1992, 'Factors Influencing Wealth Creation from Mergers and Acquisitions: A Meta-Analysis ', *Strategic Management Journal*, Vol. 13, No. 1, pp. 67-84.

Early, S 2004, 'Mergers and Acquisitions: New McKinsey Research Challenges Convential M&A Wisdom', *Strategy & Leadership*, Vol. 32, No. 2, pp. 4-11.

Eccles, R G, Lanes, K L and Wilson, T C 1999, 'Are You Paying Too Much for That Acquisition?' *Harvard Business Review*, Vol. 77, No. 4, pp. 136-146.

Eisenhardt, K 1989, 'Agency Theory: An Assessment and Review', *Academy of Management Review*, Vol. 14, No. 1, pp. 57-74.

Ensign, P 1998, 'Interrelationships and Horizontal Strategy to achieve Synergy and Competitive Advantage in the Diversified Firm', *Management Decision*, Vol. 36, No. 10, pp. 657-668.

Everitt, B 1992, *The Analysis of Contingency Tables*, London - New York - Tokyo - Melbourne - Madras, Chapman & Hall.

Fisher, R 1935, 'The Mathematical Distributions Used in the Common Tests of Significance', *Econometrica*, Vol. 3, No. 4, pp. 353-365.

Gerdes, J 2000, *Post Merger Integration: Eine empirische Untersuchung zum Integrationsmanagement*, University Münster, PhD Thesis, pp. 266

Goold, M and Campbell, A 1998, 'Desperately Seeking Synergy', *Harvard Business Review*, Vol. 76, No. 5, pp. 131-143.

Grant, R M and Jammine, A P 1988, 'Performance Differences between the Wrigley/Rumelt Strategic Categories', *Strategic Management Journal*, Vol. 9, No. 4, pp. 333-346.

Hall, G and Howell, S 1985, 'The Experience Curve from the Economist's Perspective', *Strategic Management Journal*, Vol. 6, No. 3, pp. 197-212.

Harrison, J, Hall, E, and Nargundkar R 1994, 'Resource Allocation as an Outcropping of Strategic Consistency: Performance Implications', *Academy of Management Journal*, Vol. 36, No. 5, pp. 1026-1051.

Harrison, J S, Hitt, M A, Hoskisson, R E and Ireland, R D 1991, 'Synergies and Post-Acquisition Performance: Differences versus Similarities in Resource Allocations', *Journal of Management*, Vol. 17, No. 1, pp. 173-190.

Hitt, M, Harrison, J, Ireland, R D and Best, A 1998, 'Attributes of Successful and Unsuccessful Acquisitions of US Firms', *British Journal of Management*, Vol. 9, No. 2, pp. 91-114.

Hofmann, E 2004, *Strategisches Synergie- und Dyssynergiemanagement*, University Darmstadt, PhD Thesis, pp. 378

Hofmann, E 2005, 'Realisierung von Synergien und Vermeidung von Dyssynergien', *Controlling*, No. 08-09/2005, pp. 483-489.

Hofstede, G 1991, *Culture and organizations: Software of the Mind*, London, McGraw-Hill.

Homburg, C and Bucerius, M 2006, 'Is Speed of Integration really a Success Factor of Mergers and Acquisitions? An Analysis of the Role of Internal and External Relatedness', *Strategic Management Journal*, Vol. 27, No. 4, pp. 347-367.

Hoskisson, R E, Hitt, M A, Johnson, R A and Moesel, D D 1993, 'Construct Validity of an Objective (Entropy) Categorical Measure of Diversification Strategy', *Strategic Management Journal*, Vol. 14, No. 3, pp. 215-235.

Houston, J and Ryngaert, M 1996, 'The Value Added by Bank Acquisitions: Lessons from Wells Frago's Acquisition of First Interstate', *Journal of Applied Corporate Finance*, Vol. 9, No. 2, pp. 74-82.

Howell, R A 1970, 'Plan to integrate your Acquisitions', *Harvard Business Review*, Vol. 48, No. 6, pp. 66-76.

IMAP 2008, *Annual Report 2008*, <http://www.imap.com>, accessed 8 October 2009, pp. 1-34.

Iversen, G and Norpoth, H 1987, *Analysis of Variance*, Sage.

John, C and Harrison, J 1999, 'Manufacturing-based Relatedness, Synergy, and Coordination', *Strategic Management Journal*, Vol. 20, pp. 129-145.

Keats, B 1990, 'Diversification and Business Economic Performance Revisited: Issues of Measurement and Causality', *Journal of Management*, Vol. 16, No. 1, pp. 61-72.

Kitching, J 1967, 'Why do Mergers Miscarry?' *Harvard Business Review*, Vol. 45, No. 6, pp. 84-101.

Kline, R 2005, *Principles and Practice of Structural Equation Modeling*, New York, The Guildford Press.

Kode, G V M, Ford, J C and Sutherland, M M 2003, 'A Conceptual Model for Evaluation of Synergies in Mergers and Acquisitions: A Critical Review of the Literature', *South African Journal of Business Management*, Vol. 34, No. 1, pp. 27-38.

KPMG 1999, *Unlocking Shareholder Value: The Keys to Success*, <http://www.kpmg.com>, accessed 28 August 2007, pp. 1-24.

KPMG 2006, *The Morning After - Driving for Post Deal Success*, <http://www.kpmg.com>, accessed 8 September 2007, pp. 1-14.

Lamont, O A and Polk, C 2001, 'The Diversification Discount: Cash Flows versus Returns', *Journal of Finance*, Vol. 56, No. 5, pp. 1693-1721.

Larsson, R and Finkelstein, S 1999, 'Integrating Strategic, Organizational and Human Resource Perspectives on Mergers and Acquisitions: A Case Study of Synergy Realization', *Organization Sciences* Vol. 10, No. 01-02/1999, pp. 1-25.

Lechner, H 2007a, *Negative Synergien bei Unternehmenszusammenschlüssen*, Meidenbauer.

Lechner, H 2007b, '*Synergiemanagement und Synergiecontrolling bei M&A-Projekten*', Conference Paper VWA - TU München, January 2007.

Lechner, H and Meyer, A 2003, 'Quantifizierung von Synergiepotentzialen bei Unternehmenszusammenschlüssen', *M&A Review*, No. 08-09/2003, pp. 311-316.

Lubatkin, M 1983, 'Mergers and the Performance of the Acquiring Firm', *Academy of Management Journal*, Vol. 8, No. 2, pp. 218-225.

Lubatkin, M 1987, 'Merger Strategies and Stockholder Value', *Strategic Management Journal*, Vol. 8, No. 1, pp. 39-53.

Lubatkin, M 1993, 'Construct Validity of Some Unweighted Product-count Diversification Measures', *Strategic Management Journal*, Vol. 14, pp. 433-449.

Manne, H 1965, 'Mergers and the Market for Corporate Control', *Journal of Political Economy*, Vol. 73, pp. 110-120.

Markowitz, H 1952, 'Portfolio Selection', *Journal of Finance*, Vol. 7, No. 1, pp. 77-92.

Montgomery, C A 1982, 'The Measurement of Firm Diversification: Some New Empirical Evidence', *Academy of Management Journal*, Vol. 25, No. 2, pp. 299-307.

Morck, R, Shleifer, A and Vishny, R 1990, 'Do Managerial Objectives Drive Bad Acquisitions?' *Journal of Finance*, Vol. 45, No. 1, pp. 31–48.

Mueller, D C and Sirower, M L 2003, 'The Causes of Mergers: Tests Based on the Gains to Acquiring Firms' Shareholders and the Size of Premia', *Managerial & Decision Economics*, Vol. 24, No. 5, pp. 373-391.

Mukherjee, T K, Kiymaz, H and Baker, H K 2004, 'Merger Motives and Target Valuation: A Survey of Evidence from CFOs', *Journal of Applied Finance*, Vol. 14, No. 2, pp. 7-24.

Nayyar, P R 1992, 'On the Measurement of Corporate Diversification Strategy: Evidence from Larger U.S. Service Firms', *Strategic Management Journal*, Vol. 13, No. 3, pp. 219-235.

Panzar, J C and Willig, R D 1981, 'Economies of Scope', *American Economic Review*, Vol. 71, No. 2, pp. 268-272.

Pautler, P 2003, '*The Effects of Mergers and Post-Merger Integration: A Review of Business Consulting Literature*', <http://www.ftc.gov/be/rt/businesreview paper.pdf>, accessed 20.12.2009

Pehrsson, A 2006a, 'Business Relatedness and Performance: A Study of Managerial Perceptions', *Strategic Management Journal*, Vol. 27, pp. 265-282.

Pehrsson, A 2006b, 'Business Relatedness Measurements, State-of-the-art and a Proposal', *European Business Review*, Vol. 18, No. 5, pp. 350-363.

Pehrsson, A 2009, '*Managerial Perception of Business Relatedness and Competitive Certainty: Impacts on Foreign Subsidiary Performance*', Annual Meeting of Academy of International Business, San Diego, California, USA, 27-30 June.

2009, <http://194.47.65.210/ehv/forskning/hogre_seminarier /2009 /Paper-for-presentation.pdf>, accessed 6 October 2009

Peteraf, M A 1993, 'The Cornerstones of Competitive Advantage: A Resource-Based View ', *Strategic Management Journal*, Vol. 14, No. 3, pp. 179-191.

Peterson, R A 1994, 'A Meta-Analysis of Cronbach's Coefficient Alpha', *Journal of Consumer Research,* Vol. 21, No. 09/1994, pp. 381-390.

Pitts, A 1980, 'Diversification through Acquisitions', *Strategic Management Journal*, Vol. 1, No. 3, pp. 293-294.

Porter, M E 1985, *Competitive Advantage: Creating and Sustaining Superior Performance*, New York, Free Press.

Porter, M E 1987, 'From Competitive Advantage to Corporate Strategy', *Harvard Business Review*, Vol. 65, No. 3, pp. 43-59.

Prahalad, C K and Bettis, R A 1986, 'The Dominant Logic: A New Linkage Between Diversity and Performance', *Strategic Management Journal*, Vol. 7, No. 6, pp. 485-501.

Punch, K 1998, *Introduction to Social Research*, London, Sage.

Ramaswamy, K 1997, 'The Performance Impact of Strategic Similarity in Horizontal Mergers: Evidence from the U.S. Banking Industry', *Academy of Management Journal*, Vol. 40, No. 3, pp. 697-715.

Rappaport, A 1986, *Creating Shareholder Value*, New York, Free Press.

Rhoades, S A 1974, 'A further Evaluation of the Effect of Diversification on Industry Profit Performance', *Review of Economics & Statistics*, Vol. 58, No. 4, pp. 557-559.

Robins, J A and Wiersema, M F 2003, 'The Measurement of Corporate Portfolio Strategy: Analysis of the Content Validity of Related Diversification Indexes', *Strategic Management Journal*, Vol. 24, No. 1, pp. 39-59.

Rodermann, M 1999, *Strategisches Synergiemanagement*, University Wiesbaden, PhD Thesis, pp. 427

Roll, R 1986, 'The Hubris Hypothesis of Corporate Takeovers', *Journal of Business*, Vol. 59, No. 2, pp. 197-216.

Ropella, W 1989, *Synergie als strategisches Ziel der Unternehmung*, University Bochum, PhD Thesis, pp. 333

Rumelt, R 1974, *Strategy, Structure and Economic Performance*, Cambridge, Harvard University Press.

Rumelt, R 1982, 'Diversification Strategy and Profitability', *Strategic Management Journal*, Vol. 3, No. 4, pp. 359-369.

Salter, M and Weinhold, W 1979, *Diversification through Acquisition: Strategies for Creating Economic Value*, New York, The Free Press.

Securities and Exchange Commission 2009, 13 May 2008, '*CF SIC Code List*', accessed 29 January 2009, from <http://www.sec.gov/info/edgar/sic codes.htm>.

Seth, A 1990, 'Value Creation in Acquisitions: A Re-Examiniation of Performance Issues', *Strategic Management Journal*, Vol. 11, pp. 99-115.

Shaver, J M 2006, 'A Paradox of Synergy: Contagion and Capacity Effects in Mergers and Acquisitions', *Academy of Management Review*, Vol. 31, No. 4, pp. 962-976.

Shleifer, A and Vishny, R W 1988, 'Value Maximization and the Acquisition Process', *Journal of Economic Perspectives*, Vol. 2, No. 1, pp. 7-20.

Singh, H and Montgomery, C A 1987, 'Corporate Acquisition Strategies and Economic Performance ', *Strategic Management Journal*, Vol. 8, No. 4, pp. 377-386.

Sirower, M 1997, *The Synergy Trap - How Companies Lose the Acquisition Game*, New York, Free Press.

Sirower, M L and Sahni, S 2006, 'Avoiding the "Synergy Trap": Practical Guidance on M&A Decisions for CEOs and Boards', *Journal of Applied Corporate Finance*, Vol. 18, No. 3, pp. 83-95.

Stewart, G 1987, 'Collinearity and Least Squares Regression', *Statistical Science*, Vol. 2, No. 1, pp. 68-84.

Stimpert, J L and Duhaime, I M 1997, 'In the Eyes of the Beholder: Conceptualizations of Relatedness held by Managers of Large Diversified Firms', *Strategic Management Journal*, Vol. 18, No. 2, pp. 111-125.

Swaminathan, V, Murshed, F and Hulland, J 2008, 'Value Creation following Merger and Acquisition Announcements: The Role of Strategic Emphasis Alignment', *Journal of Marketing Research*, Vol. XIV, February 2008, pp. 33-47.

Tharenou, P, Donohue, R and Cooper, B 2007, *Management Research Methods*, New York, Cambridge University Press.

Trautwein, F 1990, 'Merger Motives and Prescriptions ', *Strategic Management Journal*, Vol. 11, No. 4, pp. 283-295.

Tsai, W 2000, 'Social Capital, Strategic Relatedness and the Formation of Intraorganizational Linkages', *Strategic Management Journal*, Vol. 21, pp. 925-939.

Tschöke, K and Klemen, B 2010, 'M&A-Zyklus - Warten auf den Aufschwung', *M&A Review*, No. 02/2010, pp. 83-87.

Villalonga, B 2004, 'Diversification Discount or Premium? New Evidence from the Business Information Tracking Series', *Journal of Finance*, Vol. 59, No. 2, pp. 479-506.

Walker, M 2000, 'Corporate Takeovers, Strategic Objectives, and Acquiring-Firm Shareholder Wealth', *Financial Management* Vol. 29, No. 1, pp. 53-66.

Walsh, J 1988, 'Top Management Turnover following Mergers and Acquisitions', *Strategic Management Journal*, Vol. 9, pp. 173-183.

Walter, G A and Barney, J B 1990, 'Management Objectives in Mergers and Acquisitions', *Strategic Management Journal*, Vol. 11, No. 1, pp. 79-86.

Wernerfelt, B 1984, 'A Resource-based View of the Firm', *Strategic Management Journal*, Vol. 5, No. 2, pp. 171-180.

Wildemann, H 2003, 'Programm zur Realisierung von Synergien nach Mergers & Acquisitions, Teil 1', *Wirtschaftswissenschaftliches Studium*, Vol. 32, pp. 596-602.

Wöginger, H 2004, *Das Synergy-Value-Konzept: Synergien bei Mergers & Acquisitions*, University Vienna, PhD Thesis, pp. 314

Wrigley, L 1970, *Divisional Autonomy and Diversification*, Havard Business School, Cambridge, MA, Unpublished Doctoral Dissertation.

Yelle, L E 1974, 'Technological Forecasting: A Learning Curve Approach', *Industrial Management*, Vol. 16, No. 1, pp. 6-11.